CYCLING
fitness on wheels

CYCLING

fitness on wheels

JOHN WILCOCKSON

WORLD'S WORK LTD
PUBLISHED IN CONJUNCTION WITH
THE SUNDAY TIMES

Series edited by
John Lovesey,
Sports Editor, the *Sunday Times*

JOGGING
for fitness and pleasure
Cliff Temple

EVERYWOMAN
her guide to fitness
Chris Oram

FITNESS AFLOAT
rowing, sculling and canoeing
Richard Burnell

ORIENTEERING
for fitness and pleasure
Norman Harris

FITNESS ON FOOT
climbing and walking for pleasure
Peter Gillman

SWIMMING
a lifelong activity
John Lovesey

Published in Great Britain by World's Work Ltd
The Windmill Press, Kingswood, Tadworth, Surrey
In conjunction with the *Sunday Times*
Printed in Great Britain by
Richard Clay (The Chaucer Press) Ltd, Bungay, Suffolk
SBN 437 19200 8

Contents

CHAPTER ONE

Exercise Made Easier

'A little knowledge is a dangerous thing' may be one of the most hackneyed of aphorisms but it has considerable relevance to the intertwined subjects of health, fitness and exercise. The public may have been so bludgeoned by keep-fit, be-slim campaigns mounted by government departments, sports bodies and the media that the attitude of most people perhaps has been to throw up their hands in exasperation and to continue smoking 20 cigarettes a day, spending the lunch hour in the pub and sitting with their feet up in front of the television set in the evening.

They have been told it is smart to jog, or row, or play squash, or whatever. But when it comes to getting out and starting the new activity it is a battle to cast off the everyday luxuries and habits. There has to be some outside force to make them change those habits. It could be a very persuasive friend who takes you down the squash club. Or it could be more serious – your doctor has told you to get more exercise to avert possible obesity or heart trouble.

The realisation that youth is not eternal came to me one day in my late twenties. A colleague remarked at a Press conference that I looked to have put on a lot of weight. He was right. My excuse was that extra travelling and business commitments had caused me to buy a car, which had resulted in less time for exercise.

Previously, I had used a bicycle for most short-distance journeys, from one-mile trips to the shops to the 15-mile ride to the office. And I didn't think twice about what to do for holidays – it was always a cycling tour, the route planned months in advance on half-inch-to-the-mile road maps.

None of this had been a conscious effort to 'keep fit', so

it came as quite a shock when the bathroom scales showed that I had put on almost a stone in weight. It had become too easy to leave the bike in the shed when there was a car waiting outside; so I can understand how difficult it can be to give up familiar, lazy habits.

My immediate answer to the 'battle of the bulge' was quite simple. I already owned a bicycle, so I simply kept it in the back of the car and used it for a ride whenever I had a spare hour. For more regular exercise, I found that a 15-minute jog before breakfast did wonders for my breathing and also gave me a good appetite. A few months later, having married and moved to London, I began commuting by bike again. It was only three miles each way, but it was quicker (and cheaper) than using public transport, and I felt less guilty when I had to use a car.

It was during this period that I helped convince my wife that cigarettes were bad for her health (and she stopped smoking completely) and, in turn, she convinced me of the benefits of vegetarianism. We both switched to a non-meat diet. I soon became aware that there was far more to eating than simply consuming enough calories and that with a more natural, lighter intake of food, exercise became much easier. A less fatty diet improves your blood circulation, and eating 'whole' foods (such as wholemeal bread, fresh fruit and vegetables, wheatgerm and other unprocessed items) gives you the correct intake of vitamins and minerals in the most natural way possible.

We both lost a stone in weight over a period of three months, but the doctor explained that this was because our bodies had worked all the residual animal fats from our systems, whereas vegetable fats are much lighter and do not remain in the body so easily. In fact, he said, the loss in weight was a good sign, meaning that the body could function more efficiently. This was confirmed a few years later when we were both given thorough medicals (includcluding chest X-rays) prior to being issued with visas to work in the United States.

I was still not completely convinced (as you may not be) that a completely vegetarian diet would allow me to take part in a stamina-sapping competitive sport such as long-distance cycle racing. This has been proved to be the most calorie-consuming activity that exists, even more demanding than marathon running or cross-country skiing. I wondered if there would be any residual fats to call upon, so I undertook an experiment.

I would attempt to finish a 12-hour cycling time trial, even though I had not raced or trained seriously for five years. In that earlier period, every coach and every training manual said that it was essential to eat solid food such as steak before undertaking a bike race of more than two hours duration. I also knew that an unfit body needed at least 10 weeks of thorough training – probably about 2,000 miles of cycling – before it was in condition to start racing.

Having decided upon this experiment in mid-summer, there were less than eight weeks before the final 12-hour event that season, so both the traditional theories had to be thrown out of the window. However, I decided that the vegetarian regime would allow me to indulge in fairly concentrated training, because there was none of the usual 'excess weight' to eliminate. So, on three evenings a week, I rode the short distance to London's Richmond Park and pedalled as hard as I could for an hour each time. That meant about 25 miles each session (including the warm-up to the park), giving a total of about 100 miles in each week when a steadier Saturday ride was included.

Before finally deciding to go ahead with the 12-hour experiment, I entered time trials of 25 and 50 miles, and then a 100-miler the week before the '12'. After the first race (the 50-mile) I had some doubts about my plans as I had blown-up completely after the first 30 miles, barely reaching a respectable training speed over the final stretch. A gale-force wind didn't help matters in the '25' and I again finished with rubbery legs. But I was able to pace myself better over the 100 miles, even though this was more than twice the distance of any single ride undertaken that year. And it was a morale booster when the 100-mile result showed that I was only two minutes slower than a clubmate who had been racing regularly for years.

So the big day came, starting with a breakfast of muesli and fruit in the early hours before dawn. There followed a drive in the car of 100 miles in the dark to East Anglia; the fixing of wheels and battery lamps and the pumping up of tyres; and the consumption of two cheese sandwiches and a banana before reporting to the timekeeper at 5.30 a.m.

I knew that if I was to get through the next 12 hours of non-stop pedalling I would have to concentrate on a constant expenditure of energy.

Cycling is perhaps the best form of exercise for the heart and lungs, when it is performed at a steady rate (sprinting soon puts you in oxygen debt, so I was determined not to be tempted into going too fast on the easier parts of the course – downhill or with the wind). With this in mind, I set out to maintain a steady state of metabolic output, trying to replace as many calories as I burned during the first half of the day, and only calling on my reserves when I had the mental incentive of finishing the course.

The plan worked fairly well, although a very cold morning meant consuming more calories simply to keep warm. A patent, concentrated energy drink was my basic food source, supplemented with dried fruit, honey sandwiches, bananas and peaches as the day wore on. This scheme proved quite successful, and I never felt really hungry at any point in the race. The same couldn't be said for my legs, which gradually became unresponsive, not wanting to increase their output to that required on the uphill sections.

To compensate for this lassitude, I found that my mind took the pressure off. I would think about the shape of the next part of the course and work out how many more miles I had to ride before reaching the finishing circuit. I would lose my thoughts in studying the wooded countryside through which most of the route passed. And I would find myself thinking about other places and countries, and previous long-distance rides. All of these thoughts enabled me to forget about the apparent futility of cycling non-stop for 12 hours, generally going round in circles and finishing within a mile or so of the starting point.

My final total of 213 miles was not particularly noteworthy, being two miles per hour slower than the previous 12-hour event I had ridden some years before, but I felt that the experiment had been a success. On reflection, I could have added a few more miles to the total, because I had enough energy left to ride back to the car and then to drive home. I had lost less than half a stone in weight, and this was all replaced within a few days.

I am not suggesting that everyone becomes vegetarian and trains to ride a 12-hour time trial, but I think the experiment confirms the connection between diet and exercise: If you are to get the greatest benefit from cycling (or jogging or whatever), think of your diet and the exercise as being complementary. Having a large meal (particularly if it is meat-based) before an exercise session is clearly bad planning because you will feel sleepy and probably will postpone the exercise. Conversely, not eating enough would leave you feeling weak during the exercise period, thereby reducing its effectiveness.

CHAPTER TWO

Unwinding on Wheels

Just as your diet should be sympathetic to your other activities, so cycling should complement your other forms of exercise. This is one of the major arguments for riding a bike, because it is not necessary to practice cycling to the exclusion of all else. Skiers for example use cycling to strengthen their leg muscles before the winter season. And riding a bicycle is excellent remedial exercise.

For example, take the occasion when I strained the long tendon at the front of my ankle from too much jogging. It became almost impossible to walk – it looked as though I had a permanent limp – but I was able to cycle quite normally. The reason is that sitting on a bike takes the weight of your body from your legs. There are three points of contact (saddle, handlebars and pedals), with most of the weight being taken by your trunk and arms. The legs are left to perform their almost perfect circulatory exercise at the specific rate you choose. And that can be as gently as you like.

You may have read that many doctors say that regular cycling will relax you both physically and mentally. Perhaps the best time to put this theory into practice is at the end of the working day, the time when you are most screwed up with the pressures of office life and commuting. Have your things ready when you get home so that you can be on your bike within 15 minutes, having had a drink of fruit juice or water and changed into shorts or tracksuit.

Plan out a route on a road map beforehand, so that you know which direction you will be taking and roughly how long you will be gone. You will soon devise a favourite route, avoiding main roads as much as possible. As an example, here is the route I currently use, starting from my suburban home 15 miles from the centre of London:

The first two miles take me along a maze of backstreets before crossing a busy main road at some traffic lights. Within 10 minutes, previously stiff muscles have loosened and I'm ready to tackle a short hill that leads the route into a pocket of Green Belt countryside. I turn off this B-road into a meandering lane that most motorists wouldn't notice, even if it were signposted.

Unhurried, I can feel myself mentally unwinding – feeling the breeze on my face, hearing the birds singing in the hedgerows, seeing the animals in the fields . . . and probably smelling them as well.

Even if your surroundings are not so pleasant, you can leave them in the background and concentrate on manoeuvring your bicycle – clicking into the right gear for a sharp hill, riding close to the hedge to avoid a cross-wind or swooping down a winding descent on a perfect line. With practice, every movement becomes instinctive and you can then find yourself wrapped in your thoughts, barely conscious of the immediate world around you. This is when everyday troubles become insignificant and you may find yourself solving problems that had seemed impossible in your working environment.

After three miles along the narrow lane, passing two farmyards and two Norman churches, I have a choice of three routes. Continuing straight on will extend the ride to about 20 miles; turning left will reduce the distance to 10 miles; while the right turn gives the more usual 15 miles. After climbing to the highest point on the ride, this road dips past a knot of tile-hung cottages to join a busier B-road, from which I turn sharp left within 200 yards.

I brake for a tight downhill bend before giving the bike its head to swoop down and across a grassy valley to free-wheel half-way up the other side. A few stamps on the pedals takes me over the rise to continue freewheeling down to a small crossroads. I change to a lower gear before reaching it, turn right, then start to climb the steepest hill on the route.

Including such a challenge as this hill increases the value of a short ride. It is not the sort of exercise in which to engage during the first weeks of your conditioning programme, but to conquer a steep hill is a tremendous boost for your morale when your muscles are feeling stronger.

Climbing a long hill can be treated as a technical test – engaging bottom gear, remaining in the saddle, breathing evenly and settling into a steady rhythm of pedalling. Or, if you are feeling particularly strong, imagine it is a race and sprint up the final section to fully extend your breathing capacity.

After *my* hill, there remain four more miles to reach home, the last mile all downhill. The ride has taken less than an hour, but it is probably the most valuable hour of the day.

For family rides, when the social aspect is as important as the exercise, choose a much flatter route and one that avoids traffic as much as possible. The ideal is a specially built cycle way, cross-country trail or park road closed to motor vehicles. There are increasing numbers of such facilities, with canal towpaths and abandoned railways being prime examples. These bike-only tracks are popular in many European countries and in North America, particularly when the family's bicycles can be transported by car to the start of the trail.

If you are lucky enough to live in a town which has built (or is planning) special bikeways, then make maximum use of them for shopping trips and short rides with the family. These cyclist-only routes provide the perfect environment for learning the rudiments of safe cycling. Untroubled by the presence of motor vehicles, you will quickly iron out your initial wobbles and gain confidence to tackle roads that are busy with traffic.

Once mastered, the bicycle is the ideal means of transport in crowded city centres. For trips up to five miles, it is invariably quicker (and cheaper) than public transport. There is no 'waiting for the next bus', no parking problems and you have instant door-to-door transport. On holiday, in a foreign town perhaps, a hired bicycle will provide you with an independence that is not otherwise possible. With a road map as guide you can explore even a large city in the course of a day's cycling. Furthermore you will find that pedalling is far less tiring than walking, which allows you to concentrate on what you are seeing and experiencing, rather than getting that travel-weary feeling common to most vehicle-bound tourists.

This travel-weary phenomenon has been confirmed by scientific experiment. A study published for example by the *Scientific American* magazine in 1973 showed that a walker will consume five times as much energy as a cyclist in travelling the same distance. The cyclist, in fact, emerged as the most efficient user of energy 'among all travelling animals and machines'. The runner-up in this efficiency table, incidentally, was a swimming salmon, using 2½ times as much energy, based on calories consumed per gramme of body weight.

One reason for the bicyclist's almost perfect locomotion is that progress is maintained when you freewheel, even along a flat road, when no physical energy is being used. And energy stored by the machine during a downhill run will help your intitial progress up a following hill. The fact that your body weight is being supported, allowing your legs (which possess the most powerful muscles in your body) to put all their power into rotating the pedals, which is efficiently converted into forward motion, is another reason.

The bicycle's unique characteristics help make cycling an excellent endurance-type activity. This was revealed by the American Dr Kenneth Cooper in his famous book on aerobics, meaning the 'with oxygen' exercises that condition the heart, lungs and muscles. He conducted a series of tests to establish minimum weekly targets for aerobic activity – walking, jogging, swimming and cycling being recommended.

In cycling terms, the minimum is met by a three-mile ride in less than 11½ minutes, twice a day, five days a week. Such a target can easily be achieved by cycling to your place of employment, if it is a minimum of three miles each way. An alternative would be a 10-mile ride in less than 40 minutes, three times a week. This could be the relaxing, evening ride mentioned earlier.

This amount of cycling is within the capabilities of any able-bodied person, whatever their age. Regular cycling can safely begin when a child is mature enough to be accompanied on the road by a parent or responsible teenager. This could be as young as five years old, an age at which children love trying new activities and will see cycling as an adventure. There is probably no upper limit to riding a bike, and it is quite common for cyclists in their nineties to continue regular riding.

Two examples will help illustrate this ageless quality of cycling as an exercise. In the United States, it has become something of a graduation to cycle across America from the Atlantic to the Pacific seaboard, a distance of nearly 3,000 miles. Many family groups have been successful, the youngest children under their own steam being a nine-year-old girl and an eight-year-old boy. At the other end of the age scale, there are hundreds of over-forties in Britain who compete in long-distance races organised by the Veterans Time Trial Association (VTTA). The older riders often have an advantage, because the events are based on the time by which a rider betters the 'standard' at his (or her) age. In 1978, the VTTA 100-mile championship was won by 73-year-old Arthur Wilkins, who covered the distance in 5 hours 6 minutes 7 seconds, more than an hour faster than his 'standard'. The photo section in this book captures the happy atmosphere of a typical VTTA event.

Besides cutting across age barriers, cycling can also be made available to people with certain physical handicaps.

Many blind people get exercise by riding on the back seat of a tandem, where they can experience all the benefits of cycling without having to worry about steering, changing gear or stopping. Bicycles can also be adapted to facilitate normal cycling by people who do not have the use of all their limbs.

I have met cyclists who have the use of only one arm, but have continued to even race successfully by modifying their bikes so that the brakes and gears can be operated by one hand. It is also not uncommon to meet cyclists with the use of only one leg. Their answer is to ride a fixed-wheel machine, on which the pedals will turn as long as pressure is applied on one half of their revolution.

Cycling is therefore an exercise that is available to as wide a cross-section of people as any other activity. It is also a sport that produces athletes who are, it can be argued, the fittest in the world.

CHAPTER THREE

How to Consume Calories

A number of studies have evaluated the rate of consumption of calories for various activities. The following table is based on a study, 'Energy, work and leisure', published by Scottish researchers John Durnin and Reginald Passmore:

Activity	Calories burnt in 30 minutes
Tour de France cycling	600
Cross-country skiing	558
Squash	up to 546
Running at 10 mph	450
Swimming	up to 450
Sculling	420
Soccer	up to 360
Cycling at 13 mph	330
Tennis	up to 255
Badminton	190
Walking (3¾ mph)	150

Besides topping this table based on rate of calorie consumptions, long-distance racing cyclists also burn a much larger total of calories than other sportsmen. Based on the above figures, a tennis player would consume about 1,000 calories in a two-hour match; a soccer player a similar amount in a 90-minute match; a marathon runner about 2,250 calories; and the Tour de France cyclist a staggering 6,000 calories in a race of 125 miles (five hours).

In turn, the long hours of aerobic exercise (combined with bursts of anaerobic, or oxygen-debt, activity) give the racing cyclist an extremely efficient heart. It is quite common for professional cyclists to have at-rest pulse rates of less than 40 beats per minute, thus giving them a huge capacity for maintaining high work rates for extended periods. Again, a comparison can be made with other sportsmen, the following table coming from a 1963 publication, *Toward an understanding of health and physical education* by Arthur Steinhaus. This shows the heart size expressed as an index in terms of the medically recognised Herxheimer's fraction:

SPORTSMAN	HEART SIZE
Tour de France cyclist	24·8
Marathon runner	21·5
Rower	19·3
Short-distance cyclist	18·1
Middle-distance runner	18·1
Long-distance swimmer	16·4
Sprint runner	16·0

Besides these quantitative analyses, a most interesting qualitative survey was made in 1976 by American author James A. Michener for his exhaustive book *Michener on Sport*. In this, he sent out a questionnaire to dozens of people associated with sport (both actively, and as doctors and coaches) to rate a number of sports in terms of loading on the muscles, lungs and heart. They were asked to score each activity on an arbitary scale of 1 to 10, the highest score for the most demanding sport. These were the results:

ACTIVITY	SCORE
Tour de France cycling	10
Marathon running	9
Boxing	9
Basketball	8
Soccer	7
Tennis	6
Golf	1

There were many other – mainly American – sports listed, but none were regarded as demanding as Tour de France cycling. Only one activity was judged to be on a par, or even more demanding, the decathlon. This was not included in the table as it was thought too specialised, being performed by a very limited number of athletes in two days of concentrated competition.

In proportion to the number of cyclists, there are few that ever approach the high standards of the Tour de

France types. But the foregoing three tables demonstrate that cycling is one of the best forms of exercise to develop stamina and cardio-respiratory fitness. And, because of the high calorie-consumption rate, cycling for extended periods will also help you shed excess fat. So you will become slimmer as well as fitter.

One fear often expressed to me by women is that cycling will give them thighs as big as men's. I admit that this is a possibility, but not a probability if cycling is treated as a beneficial exercise and not as an all-consuming passion. And particularly if the exercise is combined with a diet that does not consist predominantly of convenience foods. It should also be realised that normal cycling (as opposed to racing) encourages the development of long, lean leg muscles, not short, bulbous ones.

Indeed, Dr Kenneth Cooper saw cycling as one of the most attractive exercises available to women. He wrote: 'Cycling is certainly ladylike, and definitely beneficial healthwise. It offers another chance for sports clothes, and is great for socialising, taking trips with your friends or your husband.' In the heyday of cycling in Victorian England, bicycling was considered a fashionable hobby for ladies. It is a fashion that is returning today.

Some of the world's most glamorous females ride bicycles for exercise and as a means of transport. Actresses like Farrah Fawcett-Majors and Susan Hampshire use cycling to keep trim, as do singers Doris Day and Helen Reddy. The royal families in Holland, Belgium and Sweden are all habitual cyclists, while it is a common sight to see attractive women pedalling around the streets of London, Paris or New York, with their jeans folded up over long boots and a shopping bag jauntily placed in their bicycle basket.

Another fear often expressed, by both men and women, is that cycling is dangerous. One statistic often quoted is that 'cycling is 10 times as dangerous as driving a car'. This was taken from a British government report, referring to figures for the mid-1970s that estimated the number of accidents per mile for each class of road user. What is not usually quoted is that the '10 times' was an upper limit to the estimate and that the distance travelled by each form of transport was estimated from road counts designed for motor vehicles.

A more rational estimate has been made by the Royal Society for the Prevention of Accidents (RoSPA), which says that cycling is about 2½ times as dangerous as motoring in rural areas and five times as dangerous in urban areas, again based on accidents *per mile*. However, cars probably travel at an average speed that is four to five times greater than the cyclist, therefore it can be justifiably argued that cycling is safer than motoring, based on accidents *per minute* travelled.

The latest figures (1977) show that the total number of accidents involving cyclists on British roads is not increasing, even though the numbers of cyclists is going up. This again indicates that cycling is far less dangerous than popularly believed. But until a truly comprehensive survey is completed to assess the distance travelled by cyclists annually, any reference to dangers involved is speculative. In the meantime, every person riding bicycles should learn to ride sensibly and safely in traffic, and remember that the most dangerous spots are junctions and that the majority of accidents are caused by motorists 'not seeing' the cyclist.

For children, learning to ride safely can be helped by entering the Cycling Proficiency Scheme that is organised by RoSPA. And further riding with parents or older children will help give them confidence in everyday road conditions. Ultimately, the cycling experience will help them enormously when it comes to learning to ride a motor bike or drive a motor car.

Conversely, adults who take up cycling as a means of exercise should find that their driving will improve. It will make them more understanding of the cyclist's problems on busy roads; and hopefully it will make them use a bike for those shorter trips when a car is not really necessary.

Learning to ride a bike properly, and how to use it for improving your health and fitness, will also help you to understand yourself as a person. It will help you to relax. It will help you improve your cardio-respiratory fitness. And it will help you become slimmer. Exercise is an essential ingredient in living a long life, and cycling is one of the most pleasant choices.

CHAPTER FOUR

Getting into Gear

The most difficult part of taking exercise is getting started. I like to start every day with 20 minutes of jogging because I know that it will clear my lungs, set the blood pumping and give me a good appetite for breakfast. I know it will do me good, but when the bedside radio turns itself on at just after 6.00 a.m., and it is raining outside, having another half-hour's shut-eye can seem much more attractive. This reaction is normally overcome by visiting the bathroom, washing my face with cold water and immediately donning a tracksuit. Thus committed, it seems easier to tie up my training shoes, to open the front door and to set off running towards the woods.

Invariably, I am fully woken up by the rush of cool, clean air against my face. The first, uphill run through an alleyway sets the blood circulating and the first, negative thoughts of the day are forgotten. I look forward to running up a long climb in the woods and sometimes being rewarded by the sun breaking through the early morning mist at the summit. Once back indoors, I take a quick shower, get dressed and then help to prepare breakfast of fresh grapefruit, mountains of wholemeal toast and freshly ground coffee. It is a perfect way to start the day and prepares you for tackling any problems that come your way. Exercise is infectious and you will find yourself walking the 1½ miles to the office instead of catching a bus, you will run up the stairs instead of taking the lift.

The commitment in cycling is to buy your first bike, or to dig out your old bicycle from the garden shed – probably washing away the dust it has collected, replacing the tyres that have perished and changing the brake cables that have rusted. You have made the commitment, but how do you begin the exercise? In the following condition programmes you will find some suggestions that, if followed, will bring you up to a fitness level that will make regular cycling a probability and more serious cycling a possibility.

Position

It can take years of trial and error to find the most effective, yet comfortable, position in which to pedal a bicycle. Many supposedly experienced cyclists adopt ungainly positions that often go uncorrected until they come into contact with a coach on a specialised training course. In order to avoid this situation, my advice is to follow these rules when fixing the location of the saddle and handlebars on your bike:

- The size of your frame should be about 11 inches (280 mm) less than the length of your inside leg, measured from crotch to floor. If you are less than 5 ft (1·52 metres), subtract 10 ins (255 mm); if taller than 6 ft (1·83 metres), subtract 12 ins (305 mm).
- Sitting on the saddle, astride the bike, both your feet should be able to just touch the ground. When pedalling, there should be a slight bend at the knee when your foot is at its lowest point. That sets the saddle's height.
- A rough rule to position the saddle in the forwards–backwards direction is to have the front (or peak) of the saddle about 2½ inches (63 mm) behind an imaginary vertical line through the bottom bracket axle. A more accurate check is to sit on the saddle, with the bike stationary, and one foot on its pedal. Turn the cranks until they are horizontal (the foot will be in its most forward position): The centre of your knee joint should be vertically above the pedal axle. Check this with a plumb line if possible.
- The central section of the handlebars should be level with, or lower than, the peak of the saddle. They will probably be both at the same height for touring, but the

FRAME SIZE AND POSITION

1. Chainstay: Length less than 20 ins (50 cm) on racing bike; longer for touring frames to allow for fitting mudguards and to give smoother ride.

2. Seat tube: This dimension is the frame size. Less than 20 ins (50 cm) for riders shorter than 5 ft (1·5 metres); more than 24 ins (60 cm) for riders taller than 6 ft (1·8 metres). Normal sizes 21, 22, 23 inches.

3. Seat angle: Normally 72 degrees; steeper for racing, 73 or 74; less for touring, 71 or 72.

4. Top tube: Popular frames have this length equal to seat tube length (so-called 'square' frame). Top tube longer for person with longer body.

5. Saddle height: Level with handlebars or up to 3 ins (7·5 cm) higher for racing (average height person).

6. Handlebar stem: (or extension) This dimension is longer the taller the person.

7. Fork rake: This distance is short for racing frame (less than 2 ins, 5 cm) and longer for touring, in order to give more comfortable ride.

Drawing by John Grimwade

bars will be perhaps $2\frac{1}{2}$ inches (63 mm) lower in the racing position.

- The distance between the front of the saddle and the back edge of the handlebars should be roughly equal to the measurement from the back of your elbow to the tip of your middle finger. In the riding position, check that your knees just touch the insides of your elbows when pedalling . . . if not, you will need a shorter (or longer) handlebar stem (or extension).
- The width of your handlebars should be equal to, or slightly less than, the distance between your shoulders. If too narrow or too wide, you will almost certainly suffer from back or shoulder ache.
- On 'drop' handlebars, the brake levers should be fitted so that the 'hoods' are almost horizontal, and not sticking upwards as is commonly seen.
- To pedal effectively, and comfortably, the balls of your feet should be directly over the pedal axles. If toe clips are fitted, there should be a gap of $\frac{1}{2}$ inch (12 mm) between the end of the clip and the front edge of your shoe.

* * *

What to wear

You wear clothes for four reasons in cycling: to protect the body from the elements; to maintain body temperature; to prevent injury (or chafing) at the three areas of contact (hands, feet and seat); and to give a smart appearance. As with most sports, cycling has evolved a sophisticated range of clothing for racing, training and touring; forget about these unless you progress to the more serious aspects of the activity.

For beginners, the following suggestions should prove useful, but the final choice will depend on your own standards of dress and fashion:

Upper body. Wear at least two layers of clothing. In summer, this could be a tee-shirt under a light sweater or tracksuit top; or a vest under a sports shirt. In winter, use clothing with thicker fabrics, with a second sweater or zipped windcheater on top. In cold weather, choose two long-sleeved, light sweaters in preference to one thick jumper. The layer of air trapped between the two items of clothing will act as an insulation cushion.

Waist. To avoid restricted circulation or discomfort, do not wear a tight belt around your waist or a tight elastic waistband. Keep the elastic as loose as possible, or use braces like the racing cyclists. To avoid cold air getting at the small of your back, the undervest should be long enough to cover the area when bent over in the normal cycling position.

Legs. Aching knees is one of the most common complaints among cyclists, the aches being caused either by mechanical means (a bent pedal, for instance) or physical (muscle strain through using too high gears, perhaps). Another reason is exposure to cold draughts of air. Therefore, I advise you to keep your knees covered unless the air temperature is more than 20° C (68° F), when you can wear shorts.

Tracksuit bottoms are comfortable to wear and they are usually made of a stretchy type of material that is ideal for cycling. Jeans are not comfortable to use, denim being a stiff material and the seam on the seat tends to cut into you. This can cause problems such as cystitis in women, so wear trousers (or shorts) that do not have a thick seam. The specialised cyclist's item is a pair of nylon or woollen shorts with a sewn-in chamois leather seat which has butted seams, thus reducing the chances of chafing.

Do not wear your everyday clothes for trips that are much longer than five miles (8 km) as you will find that you will sweat too much and trousers will start to wear in the seat. In winter, it may be necessary to wear waterproof overtrousers.

Feet. Shoes should be thick-soled, but not too broad. Some training shoes are ideal, although it is a good idea to buy a pair of proper cycling shoes as they are designed for the job. It is possible to buy nylon/plastic overshoes, which serve the double purpose in winter of protecting your shoes and forming an extra layer of insulation for warmth. With this in mind, it is better to wear two pairs of thinner socks in cold weather, rather than one thick pair. In summer, wear at least one pair of ankle socks to avoid chafing by your shoes.

Hands. In warm weather, it is not necessary to wear gloves, but many cyclists prefer to wear so-called track mitts (like open-backed driving gloves) that keep the palms clean and act as padding, as well as giving a good grip. In winter, wear woollen gloves that completely cover the wrists. Ski-type mittens are good protection against very cold weather.

Head. Protecting the head from possible injury in a crash is not a legal obligation and cyclists are divided about the problem. Some think that the chances of crashing and hitting your head are slim, and do not wear a protective helmet, while others think the slight risk justifies the protection. The Americans have been subject to heavy advertising and publicity on wearing helmets, consequently most cyclists there do wear them. The trend has started to infiltrate into Great Britain.

My belief is that there are greater dangers to the head from normal weather. A head exposed to hot sunshine for long periods in the summer should be protected by some form of headwear – a cotton cycling hat or cap. In winter, body heat will escape quickly through your skull unless you wear an item such as ski hat or woollen pom-pom hat. If you have to ride in below-freezing weather, then a balaclava helmet, that also covers your ears, is advisable.

To protect the eyes from bright sunshine or from cold winds, some people prefer to wear sun glasses. It is as important to apply some form of barrier cream or suntan lotion, especially if your skin is unused to exposure to strong winds.

* * *

You should now have a good impression of what you should wear for cycling and what type of bicycle to ride, and how to adjust it to find your ideal riding position. The next stage is how to learn to ride the bike, and how to use it to improve your fitness and assimilate the various techniques that make cycling such a pleasant leisure pursuit.

It is important that you do not put too much pressure on your body (muscles, heart, lungs) before it is ready for it, so the following schedules are designed to develop your strength at a gentle rate.

As with any exercise programme, the over-thirty-fives should go to their doctor before starting and have a full check-up.

BEGINNERS

If you have never ridden a bicycle in your life – or if it has been many years since you last cycled – then this schedule is for you. For the first two weeks, take your bike to a local park if there is no quiet road near your home. The initial aim is to develop confidence in balancing and then going on to build up pedalling speed, at the same time raising the saddle height towards the optimum riding position. To start, you should be able to sit astride the bike, on the saddle, with both your feet planted firmly on the ground. If you have a friend or spouse who will be able to help, so much the better. If they can run alongside during your first few attempts at riding, holding just the back of the saddle to guide you, then you will probably adapt more quickly to the sensation of cycling than if left to your own devices.

After the first week, you should have enough confidence to ride up to one mile on your own. If not, undertake a further week of practising before starting the next phase of the schedule. This next stage (weeks **2** and **3**) of riding should be done on a small circuit (perhaps a mile round), so that you are turning left all the time and not having to turn in the road (or turn right). Again, it will build up your confidence to have someone riding alongside you (or behind), so that you are not worrying about other vehicles on the road. Ideally, this circuit should also be in a park or on roads closed to motor traffic.

It is suggested in the schedule that, except at weekends, alternate days be devoted to some other form of exercise. If you already play a game such as tennis or squash, then this would do as well as the suggested walking or jogging. The idea is to get you thinking of exercise as a regular daily habit, and helping to tone up your muscles and breathing in the process.

WEEK 1

Sunday	30 minutes practice – balancing and freewheeling (a slight downhill slope will make initial efforts easier)
Monday	15 minutes walking, or mixed jogging and walking
Tuesday	20 minutes practice – balancing and freewheeling
Wednesday	As Monday
Thursday	As Tuesday
Friday	As Monday, Wednesday
Saturday	30 minutes practice – balancing and pedalling (a quiet road in a park is the best place to ride)
Total for week:	Two hours of cycling practice, 45 minutes exercise

WEEK 2

Sunday	5 km (3 miles) of riding practice around a left-handed circuit

Monday	20 minutes walking, or mixed jogging and walking
Tuesday	As Sunday
Wednesday	As Monday
Thursday	As Sunday, Tuesday
Friday	As Monday, Wednesday
Saturday	8 km (5 miles) of riding practice around circuit
Total for week:	23 km (14 miles) practice riding; 1 hour other exercise

WEEK 3

Sunday	10 km (6 miles) of cycling (in 40 minutes) around circuit
Monday	20 minutes other exercise
Tuesday	8 km (5 miles) cycling (in 30 minutes) around circuit
Wednesday	As Monday
Thursday	As Tuesday
Friday	As Monday, Wednesday
Saturday	10 km (6 miles) of cycling (in 35 minutes) around circuit
Total for week:	36 km (22 miles) cycling ($2\frac{1}{4}$ hours); 1 hour other exercise

WEEK 4

(*Miss this if you are over 50 and go to age group schedule*)

Sunday	13 km (8 miles) cycling on quiet roads open to other traffic (50 minutes)
Monday	20 minutes other exercise
Tuesday	10 km (6 miles) cycling on circuit (35 minutes)
Wednesday	As Monday
Thursday	As Tuesday
Friday	As Monday, Wednesday

Saturday	13 km (8 miles) cycling on quiet roads (45 minutes)
Total for week:	46 km (28 miles) cycling (2¾ hours); 1 hour other exercise

WEEK 5

Sunday	16 km (10 miles) cycling on quiet roads (60 minutes)
Monday	20 minutes other exercise
Tuesday	10 km (6 miles) cycling on circuit (30 minutes)
Wednesday	As Monday
Thursday	As Tuesday
Friday	As Monday, Wednesday
Saturday	13 km (8 miles) cycling on quiet roads (40 minutes)
Total for week:	49 km (30 miles) cycling (2 hours 40 minutes); 1 hour other exercise

WEEK 6

(*Miss this out if over 35 and go to age group schedule*)

Sunday	20 km (12 miles) cycling on quiet roads (60 minutes)
Monday	20 minutes other exercise
Tuesday	12 km (7½ miles) cycling on circuit (30 minutes)
Wednesday	As Monday
Thursday	As Tuesday
Friday	As Monday, Wednesday
Saturday	16 km (10 miles) cycling on quiet roads (45 minutes)
Total for week:	60 km (37 miles) cycling (2¾ hours); 1 hour other exercise

After six weeks, the beginner should be at a stage when

riding speeds of 12–15 mph (20–24 km/hr) have become acceptable. You should not be using high gears. Keep to the middle and bottom gears on a 3-speed bicycle, or under 70 inches (see Appendix Three) if you have derailleur gears. The aim in this first six weeks is to learn a gentle pedalling style and the rudiments of cycle riding – how to go round corners, how to brake, how to change gear, how to stop and start safely, and how to carry out basic manoeuvres in traffic.

Your saddle height should gradually be raised over the six weeks, so that you have now adopted the recommended position for cycling. If the weather is too wet for cycling for several days, go for a walk instead, and restart with the week's cycling you have missed. Do not worry about missing the odd day of cycling. It is meant to be an enjoyable progress towards fitness, not an uphill battle against the elements.

It is almost certain that the new experience of riding a bicycle will make your buttocks sore in the first few weeks; but, by the end of this preparatory stage, the aches will have probably moved to your leg muscles as they become accustomed to longer periods of pedalling. Remember that aching muscles equate with increasing fitness: blood is being pumped through your arteries to muscles that have probably not been exercised for years.

You should now be ready to continue the evolutive process of getting (and keeping) fit, as outlined in the following schedules for different age groups. I have not differentiated between men and women because the programmes suggested should be within the capabilities of either sex. This book is not aimed at cyclists who are training for competition, although someone who follows these schedules through would obtain an adequate grounding to graduate to more serious training.

As with the programme for beginners, anybody over 35 years of age should have a check-up with their doctor before starting.

UP TO 35 YEARS OF AGE

Do not begin this schedule unless you are in fairly good condition. If you are obviously overweight, or you have to catch your breath after walking up more than two flights of stairs, then start with the beginner's programme. This next phase will bring you up to a higher level of fitness, ready to maintain a constant exercise routine for the rest of your life.

WEEK 1

Sunday	10 km (6 miles) on a circuit or park roads (30 minutes)
Tuesday	10 km (6 miles) in 30 minutes (evening ride, or to and from work)
Thursday	As Tuesday
Saturday	20 km (12 miles) on quiet roads (60 minutes)
Total for week:	50 km (31 miles) in 2½ hours

(*Supplement this cycling with other exercise, such as walking or jogging on the spare days*)

WEEK 2

Sunday	16 km (10 miles) in 45 minutes (quiet roads)
Tuesday	11 km (6¾ miles) in 30 minutes (evening or commuting)
Thursday	As Tuesday
Saturday	22 km (13½ miles) in 60 minutes (quiet roads)
Total for week:	60 km (37 miles) in 2¾ hours

WEEK 3

Sunday	17 km (10½ miles) in 45 minutes (quiet roads)

Tuesday	12 km (7½ miles) in 30 minutes (evening or commuting)
Thursday	As Tuesday
Saturday	23 km (14 miles) in 60 minutes (quiet roads)
Total for week:	64 km (40 miles) in 2¾ hours

WEEK 4

Sunday	18 km (11¾ miles) in 45 minutes (quiet roads)
Tuesday	12 km (7½ miles) in 30 minutes (evening or commuting)
Thursday	As Tuesday
Saturday	24 km (15 miles) in 60 minutes (quiet roads)
Total for week:	66 km (41¼ miles) in 2¾ hours

By the end of week **4**, you should have little difficulty in maintaining an average pace of 15 mph (24 km/hr). If you find this impossible, then you continue building up fitness within the above framework of four rides a week between 30 and 60 minutes duration. A ride is best non-stop, but if you split it into two make sure that you keep warm during the halt, particularly in cold weather. You will be losing the benefit of the exercise if you have to warm up your muscles again.

Look on the suggested distances in each week as the minimum to cover. If you feel like riding further after you have followed the schedule for at least two weeks, then go ahead. But it is better to wait until you have a month's conditioning behind you before planning longer day trips.

35–50 YEARS AGE GROUP

Having had your check-up, decide what your programme is going to be. If you are badly out of shape, then do some general exercise (walking to start with) before getting into the beginner's schedule. Follow this right through unless you are already used to riding a bike. In this case, miss out the first two weeks of the beginner's schedule, to give you a four-week run-in to your age group schedule. Do not be too ambitious. Remember that you will be learning to ride a bike properly; to discipline your life to make time for exercise; and to harden up your body to the new efforts, as well as exercising the heart and lungs. It all takes time, so do not rush things.

WEEK 1

(*This will be Beginner's Week* 6)

Sunday	16 km (10 miles) in 55 minutes (quiet roads)
Tuesday	10 km (6 miles) in 28 minutes (morning or evening ride)
Thursday	As Tuesday
Saturday	13 km (8 miles) in 39 minutes (quiet roads)
Total for week:	49 km (30 miles) in 2½ hours

(*Continue other exercise on spare days*)

WEEK 2

Sunday	16 km (10 miles) in 50 minutes (quiet roads)
Tuesday	10 km (6 miles) in 26 minutes (morning or evening)
Thursday	10 km (6 miles) in 26 minutes (morning or evening)
Saturday	14 km (8½ miles) in 40 minutes (quiet roads)
Total for week:	50 km (31 miles) in 2 hours 22 minutes

WEEK 3

Sunday	20 km (12 miles) in 60 minutes (quiet roads)
Tuesday	10 km (6 miles) in 25 minutes (morning or evening)
Thursday	As Tuesday
Saturday	16 km (10 miles) in 45 minutes (quiet roads)
Total for week:	56 km (34 miles) in 2 hours 35 minutes

WEEK 4

Sunday	22 km (13½ miles) in 60 minutes (quiet roads)
Tuesday	11 km (6¾ miles) in 27½ minutes (morning or evening)
Thursday	As Tuesday
Saturday	17 km (10½ miles) in 45 minutes (quiet roads)
Total for week:	61 km (37½ miles) in 2 hours 40 minutes

WEEK 5

Sunday	24 km (15 miles) in 60 minutes (quiet roads)
Tuesday	12 km (7½ miles) in 30 minutes (morning or evening)
Thursday	As Tuesday
Saturday	18 km (11¼ miles) in 45 minutes (quiet roads)
Total for week:	66 km (41¼ miles) in 2¾ hours

OVER FIFTIES AGE GROUP

Follow the first three weeks of the beginner's schedule before moving on to this programme. It is planned for a steady build-up towards a lower minimum fitness level than previous schedules, but switch to the 35–50 age group schedule if you find this one too easy.

WEEK 1

Sunday	10 km (6 miles) in 37½ minutes (quiet roads or circuit)
Tuesday	8 km (5 miles) in 30 minutes (on circuit)
Thursday	As Tuesday
Saturday	10 km (6 miles) in 35 minutes (quiet roads)
Total for week:	36 km (22 miles) in 2 hours 12½ minutes

(*Continue other exercising on spare days*)

WEEK 2

Sunday	13 km (8 miles) in 48 minutes (quiet roads)
Tuesday	8 km (5 miles) in 27½ minutes (on circuit)
Thursday	As Tuesday
Saturday	10 km (6 miles) in 32 minutes (quiet roads)
Total for week:	39 km (24 miles) in 2¼ hours

WEEK 3

Sunday	13 km (8 miles) in 45 minutes (quiet roads)
Tuesday	8 km (5 miles) in 25 minutes (on circuit)
Thursday	As Tuesday
Saturday	10 km (6 miles) in 30 minutes (quiet roads)
Total for week:	39 km (24 miles) in 2 hours 5 minutes

WEEK 4

Sunday	14½ km (9 miles) in 45 minutes (quiet roads)
Tuesday	10 km (6 miles) in 30 minutes (evening or morning ride)
Thursday	As Tuesday
Saturday	10 km (6 miles) in 27 minutes (quiet roads)
Total for week:	44½ km (27 miles) in 2 hours 12 minutes

WEEK 5

Sunday	14½ km (9 miles) in 42½ minutes (quiet roads)
Tuesday	10 km (6 miles) in 27 minutes (morning or evening)
Thursday	As Tuesday
Saturday	10 km (6 miles) in 25 minutes (quiet roads)
Total for week:	44½ km (27 miles) in 2 hours 2½ minutes

WEEK 6

Sunday	16 km (10 miles) in 42½ minutes (quiet roads)
Tuesday	10 km (6 miles) in 25 minutes (morning or evening)
Thursday	As Tuesday
Saturday	13 km (8 miles) in 35 minutes (quiet roads)
Total for week:	49 km (30 miles) in 2 hours 7 minutes

WEEK 7

Sunday	16 km (10 miles) in 40 minutes (quiet roads)
Tuesday	10 km (6 miles) in 24 minutes (morning or evening)
Thursday	10 km (6 miles) in 24 minutes (morning or evening)
Saturday	13 km (8 miles) in 32 minutes (quiet roads)
Total for week:	49 km (30 miles) in 2 hours

* * *

If you have followed the schedules through from beginning to end, you will have been using a bicycle for 10 weeks. It has been a purposely slow build-up and it should be looked on as a preparation towards a healthier and more enjoyable life.

CHAPTER FIVE

A Life Cycle

When you have been cycling regularly for a number of weeks, you will find dramatic improvements in your breathing and circulation. You should have started to lose a few pounds and to shed some inches from round the waist. You should be feeling more relaxed and less likely to suffer from fatigue. Hopefully, you will also be helping the exercise by eating a more natural diet: cutting down on your intake of fats, perhaps cutting out sugar and eating more fresh fruit and vegetables. You will be feeling healthier.

Most of your riding so far will have been in parks or on quiet side roads or even country lanes. They are healthy places to exercise, of course; but when you start to use the bike for trips into town, you may think that the car and smoke fumes will be damaging to your health, especially as you are not enclosed like a motorist. This is a false fear as surveys carried out in Britain and the United States have shown that the level of carbon monoxide poisoning in the blood is no higher for a cyclist than it is for a pedestrian. And the level could be higher for a motorist driving in heavy traffic.

A London doctor confirmed these results by a 10-mile ride through Central London, his carbon monoxide level being about half that of motorists driving in 15 miles from the suburbs. The highest level (on a still day) was about 0·5 per cent for the cyclist – which compares with a level of 14 per cent for a smoker who gets through two packs a day. This shows that you are likely to inhale more unpleasant fumes in travelling by public transport than commuting by bicycle.

It is also much cheaper to use a bike for short everyday trips rather than using buses, trains or private cars. And it is cheaper to buy a bicycle today in real terms than ever before. Statistics for 1978 show that it took *four* days to earn enough (at the rate of the average income) to buy an average bike with three gears, which compares with more than *eight* days to buy a similar new bike in 1938.

It is also much cheaper to maintain a bike. A comparison of costs carried out by the British Cycling Bureau in 1978 showed that (for an 8-mile-a-day return journey) the annual running costs for a bicycle were £22·20, which included using public transport on 12 inclement days. The equivalent bus fares for the 239 working days of the year totalled £143·00, while the private car cost £268·00 (excluding parking fees).

If you are not sure that cycle commuting is the ideal method of travelling to work, then try it out on one day a week for a short period, when the weather is fine. You will then get an idea of how long it takes compared with your usual mode of transport. You will also discover how you feel on reaching work, and whether you feel tired (or fresher) at the end of the day. Other points to check out are where to leave the bike (take it in the building, if possible, otherwise chain it to some railings using a reliable padlock); whether it is possible to change your clothes on arrival, and how long this takes; and whether there are any side-street alternatives to the busy main-road route.

If the journey is less than five miles, it is unlikely that you will need to take a change of clothing. Plan your route to avoid really steep hills and busy intersections (there is usually an alternative), and then gradually build up the frequency of your rides. After the initial test runs, go by bike every fine day until you get into the habit of riding every day.

In the winter, you will need lights, front and rear. Battery lamps are more convenient, although they can be affected by bumpy roads and become unreliable (rattling or jumping loose). Dynamo lights are efficient, but they stop working when you stop the bike. Therefore, in heavy traffic, it is wise to wear at night a brightly coloured waistcoat (as used by motor-cyclists). You will then be clearly visible, even if your bike is not.

To protect yourself from the weather, fit your bike with full mudguards (not the so-called racing ones) and carry some form of wet-weather clothing. This could be a cape and waterproof overtrousers, with a waterproof hat that will stop water going down your neck. This clothing has the disadvantage that you will sweat more, and I usually prefer to ride through the rain and dry out at my destination. If it is a day of torrential or continuous rain then travel by some other means if you do not fancy getting wet.

Another problem you may need to overcome is carrying papers to and from the office, or any other luggage. You can buy a luggage rack for the bike and this will support a saddle bag or side panniers – all of which are copious. Alternatives are a small bag mounted on the handlebars (with a metal-framed support) and a shoulder bag. Neither of these are suitable for carrying heavy loads.

If the distance between home and place of employment is too far to cover by bike in less than an hour, you could still cycle part of the journey. It is free to transport your bike on British Rail and it is now quite common to see commuters ride their bikes to the local station, travel by train and then ride from the next station to work. Another method is to drive in by car to the suburbs of town, park your car without parking fees and then cycle the rest of the way. A folding bike can be kept in the car boot, or you can strap your bicycle to a roof rack. There are also racks on the market for specifically transporting bicycles.

* * *

Cycle commuting is not suitable for everyone, and is not necessary if you have to travel less than one mile: the walk will do you more good. The next phase in developing your use of the bicycle could be for day trips at the weekend.

Cycling into the countryside is an adventure. You discover places that you never knew existed. You will experience the joy of travelling without the confinement of a car, bus or train. You can stop where you like, use tracks that are barred to motorists and, at the end of the day, feel that you have earned the reward of a big meal.

A day trip can be as short as 20 miles or as long as 200, although the most likely distance to be covered is between 40 and 100 miles. Before setting out, decide where you are going; whether you will take food for a picnic, or eat along the way; and who you are going with, if you do not go alone. The answers will decide exactly how the trip is to be tackled.

I can still remember my first serious day trip when I was at school. A group of boys in the same form, most of whom rode their bikes to school, decided that Eastbourne would be a good destination – would I like to come along? This decided, I borrowed what I thought was a suitable bike (only later did I discover that a fixed-wheel machine with a fairly high gear was probably the least suitable). Sandwiches and fruit were packed into a small shoulder bag after breakfast and I rode off into the early morning to the rendezvous point. I believe there were six of us that made the trip.

It was exhilarating being on the road before most people were out of bed, the feeling accentuated by the sense of adventure as familiar roads were left behind. It must have been 30 miles before I first had second thoughts about the ride. The long climb over the Ashdown Forest in Sussex had me beaten and I had to push the bike to the top. The others had waited, but they were impatient to get going again and I had to suffer in silence with my feet and legs aching from the climb.

The route was continually up and down, but a following wind had helped us make good time and we were well pleased to reach the seaside before lunchtime. With our backs to the sea wall and our shoes off, we devoured our packed lunches and were soon looking round for ice creams and crisps. On reflection, we probably stayed too long on the beach before heading the 60 miles back home.

Thankfully the sun was shining and the climb past Beachy Head was worth the effort before we plunged down the hills towards Lewes. I can remember being surprised by how old the towns appeared: the little, cobbled lanes, brick and timber Tudor houses, leaded lights and square towered churches of stone. And the countryside seemed so rural, with isolated hamlets and sleepy village greens.

It was tempting to stop for tea at one of the villages, but cakes and liquid refreshment were soon burnt up and I was struggling to keep up with the others 20 miles from home. The final 10 miles are still a blur in my memory, caused by fatigue, hunger and complaining muscles. It was almost dark when I finally reached home and I think I went straight to bed I was so tired.

You could say it was a character-building trip, but such a badly planned bike ride could quite easily have put me off riding a bike ever again. Thankfully, only the good memories remained. The first mistake was to make the trip overlong. Eastbourne sounded fine, but it turned out to be a round trip of 115 miles. If I replanned the trip, now I would probably make Lewes or Newhaven the destination. I would use a bike with derailleur gears. I would take enough food so that some was kept for the journey back. And I would take a good road map so as to avoid main roads as much as possible. The one point that I would not change is the company, as riding with a group of friends helped me get through the day, especially those last few miles.

A more rational way to start day trips is to choose a destination that is familiar to you. This could be a favourite cafe or tea shop, where you know a good meal can be obtained. This should be about 15 miles from home, so that you can plan a different route back from the one going there, to give a total distance of about 35 miles. This would be a comfortable distance to cover in a morning or afternoon. For longer trips, most cycling tourists like to start early in the morning, so that they can get home comfortably before nightfall.

To progress to full tours, the next step is to go away for a weekend, stopping overnight at accommodation you have booked in advance. On such a trip you will discover a new aspect to the cycling adventure, riding through unfamiliar landscapes in a different region. There will also be a sense of achievement when you see the distance to your destination slowly decreasing on the signposts, followed by the actual arrival in another town.

For a weekend trip, take a saddlebag or panniers on the bike. Pack a change of clothes and shoes for the evening, and one for the next day's return journey. Your choice of overnight stop is unlimited. Youth hostels are normally friendly and occupy interesting old buildings. Guest houses are comfortable and you will get good value for money. And you will probably be well received at hotels.

Ask where you can store your bike in a safe place, undercover. And don't worry if you look a little travel weary when you arrive. I once arrived at a 4-star hotel in County Durham after a ride of about 11 hours across the Pennines. A porter took my pannier bags up to my room, the bike was accommodated in a lock-up garage and I then enjoyed the deepest bath I have ever seen, drying myself with the longest, heaviest towel I had ever used. Within an hour I had emerged in clean shirt, pressed trousers and polished shoes, ready for an aperitif at the bar and a meal that, I remember, ended with strawberries and cream.

Once you have spent a weekend away, next plan for a long weekend, starting out Friday afternoon for a first-night stop about 50 miles from home. The procedure will be the same for any tour, the difference with longer trips that you have to pack more frugally, taking enough clean clothes to last the whole trip. It is possible to pack enough in saddlebag and panniers for tours of up to three weeks duration.

Planning longer trips (either in Britain or overseas) is one of the pleasures during the winter, working out distances and routes on exciting looking maps. But don't take my word for it – try it yourself!

CHAPTER SIX

Choosing a Bike

The principal difference between cycling and any other popular form of exercise is that before you can start you will need a sophisticated piece of machinery. This could cost you less than £10 at the local jumble sale, or more than £1,000 at the showroom of a specialist lightweight dealer. Before you decide how far your cheque book can stretch, remember that it is your body you will be exercising not the bicycle. You will be able to get equally fit on your single-geared second-hand mount as on the multi-geared, superlight special. The difference is that the smart, new bicycle may encourage you to go cycling more frequently. It will be a status symbol to make you feel good and to impress your friends; but even the most expensive machine is worthless unless it is correctly adjusted and maintained.

I am often asked by non-cycling friends: 'What is a good make of bicycle? What sort of bike is best? How much does a good machine cost?' My answer usually goes like this: 'There are many good makes, as such, but the important thing is whether it has a lightweight frame that has been well made and well finished off. Next, look at the components. Alloy ones are lighter, will not rust, but will be more expensive. Steel ones will be heavier, but cheaper. You could buy a satisfactory lightweight production model for less than £100, but one costing twice that will probably be more efficient, more comfortable and easier to maintain.'

In other words, you must decide what you want to get out of cycling before choosing the type, and price, of bicycle that will suit your purposes. Many people are discouraged by cycling being 'hard work', simply because

SPECIAL
REPORT

A Veterans Time Trial

A photographic essay by Mark Ellidge of the national 50-miles championship of the Veterans Time Trial Association organised by the Wessex Group and held on a course in the New Forest. Similar events – at distances from 25 miles to 24 hours – are held every weekend between March and October throughout Great Britain.

Adapted from a feature that originally appeared in The Sunday Times.

A line is chalked on the road, a warning sign placed by the kerb and another time trial for veteran cyclists (over-40s) is underway. Similar events are held every weekend throughout Britain. This one is the 50 miles national championship of the Veterans Time Trial Association. There are 82 competitors, average age 56, starting at one-minute intervals to race 'entirely alone and unassisted' against the watch. Although the oldest is 70, the youngest 40, everyone has a chance of success. Standard times (something like a par in golf) are established for each age. The winner is the one who beats his 'standard' by the widest margin.

On the B3347 two miles south of Ringwood, Hampshire, first man is due to start at 6.01 am. Timekeeper Joan Attenborough and her assistant (*above*) settle back for the morning, waiting to time each rider in after completing the out-and-back course. In attendance at this event was Dr Andrew Loughran, who measured riders' pulse rate, blood pressure and recovery rate. Man being tested (*right*) is Rex Webber, then 65, whose pulse at rest was 50. His final time: 2hr 18min 8sec.

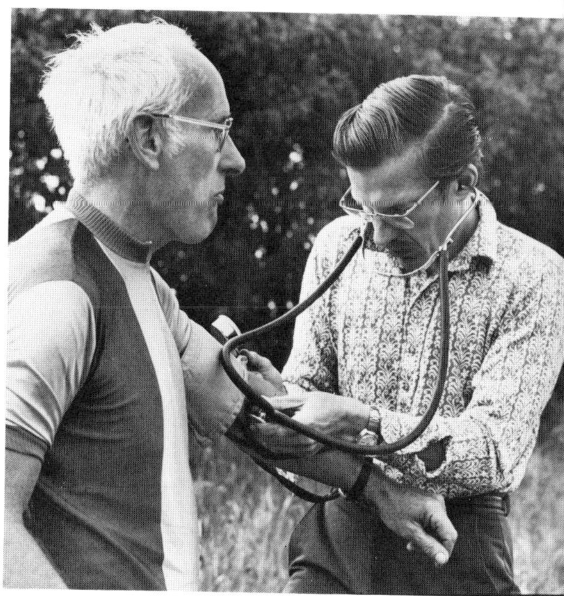

'Which number are you?' is the greeting as two competitors look for their plastic number plates, which fix to their bike frames. The fast men are usually numbered on the zeroes – 10, 20, 30 . . . One such seed is 52-year-old Ken Jones (*right*), who has cycled regularly for nearly 40 years. His pulse was 56. His time 2:14 : 02.

Listening out for the '5–4–3–2–1–go' signal is the oldest man in the race, Stan Harvey (*left*), a retired cabinet maker from Croydon He has been training 400 miles a week and as a result, is riding faster than he has done for 14 years Why? 'I'm fitter. Before I retired standing all day did the old legs no good,' he explained. Out of the saddle up one of the New Forest hills (*above*) is Roy Stubbs, 45, a mine safety engineer who had neglected exercise for 19 years He has lost four stones in weight and reduced his pulse to 60. His race time: 2:20:40. Watching the men today is attractive Jan Ashby from Bristol (*right*), of the Gordano Valley Club, one of more than 100 women in the VTTA's 3,000-plus membership.

They are veterans in name but not in attitude. The most expensive of Italian equipment graces the bike of Owen Blower (*above*), a Leicester knitware manufacturer, who made a comeback to the sport after 15 years off the bike. At 44, he records 2:00:29. His best '50' time is 1:54:00. Not so rapid is Major Harry Keates (*right*), 66, who first rode 100 miles in a day when he was eight. He helped form the Army Cycle Union during 32 years in the forces. His pulse: 70. Time: 2:33:46.

Some veterans, like 62-year-old Ivor Jones (*above*) from the VTTA's West group, stay faithful to equipment they used in their youth. His bike has fixed wheel, cottered steel cranks and one simple side-pull brake.

Bill Suttie, 56, of Bournemouth Jubilee Wheelers (*right*), is a typical time trial enthusiast. He has few pretensions to winning. His enjoyment comes from competing every weekend with cyclists of similar outlook on life. His ambitions are limited to bettering his age standard time (he will have new ones to aim for each year) or improving on his personal best for the distance. Perhaps most of all, there is the satisfaction of completing an accurately measured course at a respectably fast pace. After passing the chequered flag (*below*), his time will be marked on the result board for all to see and, over a gentlemanly cup of tea, he will compare notes on the day's ride with his peers.

'I'll be like a dog with two tails all week,' enthuses Stan Harvey at the end of his ride. His time of 2:22:59 beats the 70-year-olds' standard by a wider margin than anyone else can beat theirs and he's declared the 50-miles champion. Dr. Loughran was most impressed: 'As a breed, these cyclists are fitter than footballers and rugby players, and as fit as athletes less than half their age. After a hard ride, in heat which dehydrates and depletes, Stan Harvey's pulse showed the most complete and sustained recovery.' The champion's pulse is 45 at rest, and recovered from 120 to 60 within 15 minutes of finishing.

their bike is heavy or the wrong size. Therefore, buying an unsuitable machine is as bad as not buying a bicycle at all. You would be better off choosing some other form of exercise.

To overcome this problem of what to choose, make efforts to try out as many different types of bicycle as possible before making a purchase. Perhaps you will be able to borrow a friend's bike for a few days; this would give you a standard with which to compare a bicycle that you may try out in the showroom. Another idea is to hire one (or more) machines with which to make a comparison.

Bicycle hire is a perfect, if rather expensive, method of testing the different types of machine. A week of riding a small-wheeled 'shopper', followed by a week with a 10-speed sports model, will give you a good insight into the the relative performance and characteristics of the two most popular types of modern bicycle. Do not attempt, at this stage, to use either bike for extended touring trips. Make best use of the hire period for normal, about-town riding, with perhaps a longer ride into the countryside at the weekend.

Before leaving the hire shop, ask the assistant to help you adjust the height of the saddle and handlebars so that you have the most comfortable position for your trial run. Also, if you are not sure, ask how to repair a puncture, how to remove a tyre from the rim and what type of valve is fitted. If you are still unsure, ask the assistant for a spare tube, which can be used instead of repairing a puncture. It is always good policy to carry a spare (essential if your bike has sewn-up, tubular tyres, the type used for racing).

Once you have decided what type of bicycle will suit you best, the next choice is whether to invest in a brand new one, or whether to start with a good second-hand machine. If you haven't ridden a bike for several years, or if you are a complete newcomer, my advice is to start with a second-hand bicycle. This will give you the opportunity of learning the various skills of cycling without you having to worry overmuch about chipping the paintwork or damaging the wheels. You will also get to know what you like (or dislike) about a particular type of bicycle – perhaps the gears are too high, the saddle is too spongy or the frame is too big. It is much better to discover any such features before spending a small fortune on an unsuitable machine.

The second-hand bike is best bought from a recognised dealer, who will have checked it over and adjusted it properly before selling. If you are confident that you know how to check it yourself, look for a bicycle on sale in the classified columns of a local paper or in a specialised magazine. And, if you are not sure, take someone with you who does know what to look for.

The type of bicycle you buy will depend on what type of cycling you plan, whether you will be using flat or hilly roads, how often it will be used and what will be the longest trips you plan to undertake. There has never been a wider range of bicycles on the market, whatever your price-bracket, but check out the latest information on models available before paying out money.

It is still possible to buy old-fashioned, big-wheeled heavyweights, but current opinion favours machines that are lighter and multi-geared. In 1977, more than 40 per cent of the one million new bicycles sold in Great Britain were of the so-called 'sports' type. This popularity for a more streamlined machine was reflected in a Consumers' Association *Which?* report (August 1978) that dealt with bicycles for children in the 11–16 years age group.

Almost without exception, the teenagers in the survey 'who rode the bikes . . . liked drop-handlebar bikes best'. The recommended 'best buy' was a 5-speed model with racing-type saddle and handlebars. This was 'very well liked' by the children who 'thought it fast, handled well and enjoyed riding it'. And most of them said that they wanted their next bike to be similar to this.

These opinions were put into a quantitative form by an American study conducted by the USA's National Safety

Council (published in *Traffic Safety*, October 1976). It was found that riders of bicycles with five (or more) gears travelled more in busy areas, travelled greater distances and had fewer accidents per 1,000 miles travelled. The accident rate for these riders was exactly half that for riders of single-speed bikes, the figures being as follows:

BICYCLE TYPE	**ACCIDENT RATE (per 1,000 miles)**
1 gear	0·72
3 gears	0·54
5 gears (or more)	0·36

There are probably two reasons for the sports type being safer. The lighter bike, with a wide choice of gears, is easier to ride and the rider has greater acceleration potential to avoid dangerous situations. And more experienced riders will normally progress to more expensive, lighter machines.

It is generally true that cheaper bikes are heavy, which is the reason why a second-hand lightweight is a better buy. One exception to the rule is the small-wheeled fun bike which has bench-type seat, high-riser handlebars and thickly treaded rear wheel. This is not inexpensive, but it can weigh more than 40 lb (18 kilograms), a prohibitive weight for easy cycling.

Ignoring such extreme examples, it is possible to draw up a direct connection between weight and price.

WEIGHT (kg)	**WEIGHT (lbs)**	**PRICE RANGE (1978 values)**	**TYPE**
Less than 10	Less than 22	High (£200 and up)	Racing, or high-speed touring and commuting
10–14	22–31	Medium high (£125–£200)	Long-distance commuting, touring and racing
14–18	31–40	Medium (£60–£125)	Short-distance commuting and touring
More than 18	More than 40	Low (less than £60)	Too heavy for serious cycling

The reason for there being such a wide variation in the weight of bicycles that, on first appearance, are the same size and shape is the choice of frame tubing and metal accessories. The heavier bike has plain gauge tubing (made of regular steel and of the same thickness throughout its length) and is fitted with steel equipment (chain wheel, hubs, rims, brakes, handlebars, pedals and spokes). In contrast, the lightweight has butted tubing (made of alloy steel, with a narrower gauge, except for the thicker – butted – ends) and light alloy equipment.

Within each weight category, as outlined, there can be a wide variation in quality of components. The more reputable, race-proven equipment is manufactured in Italy, France and Japan. These countries also produce the best tubing, along with Great Britain.

Frame

The biggest difference between a cheap and an expensive bicycle is the frame's construction. The cheap bike will have a frame that is mass produced, with the minimum of quality controls and tolerance checks. The expensive frame will be hand-built by a skilled craftsman, with each tube and lug being hand-filed to make a perfect fit before the joints are formed with low-temperature brazing. Such laborious and exacting work makes for a frame that is immensely strong and resilient: essential properties for a bike that is to be used for racing or long-distance touring.

The traditional, diamond-shaped frame owes its strength to the triangulation of the main components. The basic dimensions (see drawing on page 25) can be varied considerably to give made-to-measure machines. Classically, the seat and top tubes will be the same length and the head and seat angles will be equal. For touring, the angle will be about 72 degrees. It will be steeper for racing: up to 75 degrees. Another difference between touring and racing frames is that the tourer will have a longer front-fork rake, which ensures a more comfortable ride. If the front forks were straight, every imperfection on the road surface would be transmitted directly to the rider's arms and shoulders.

Small-wheeled, folding and ladies' bicycles all have open frames, which are inherently weaker than diamond frames. This should be borne in mind before choosing a new bike, especially by a person who is above average height. One exception to this is the strengthened version of the Bickerton portable bike that in 1978 passed the stringent regulations of the American consumer products board. This frame is based on a box profile aluminium girder, from which it gains its rigidity. But the long length of seat pillar required by a tall rider is a problem inherent in all folding bikes.

For children, there is a wide choice of bikes that utilise reduced sizes of the full diamond frame. The small-wheeled bike has some advantages for quickly growing children in that the saddle can be progressively raised without entirely replacing the bike.

Cranks and chainset

There are two types of cranks: steel ones which fit to the axle by means of wedge-shaped cotter pins and alloy cotterless ones, which push on to a splined axle and are fixed by a bolt that screws into the axle end. It is vital that both types be fitted accurately for efficient service. If not, the cranks could work loose, causing wear to the axle in the process. This can be a particularly expensive process with cotterless cranks.

If you want a bike for serious cycling (racing, long-distance touring) then the lighter cotterless cranks are preferable. Most versions have easily fitted, interchangeable chain rings that are fixed by small nuts to the right-hand crank. This allows two (or three) chain rings to be fitted, thus providing a wide range of variable gears.

Gears

There are four separate methods of gearing a bicycle: by direct, fixed wheel; by a single, freewheel; by an epicyclic hub gear; and by derailleur gears.

The fixed gear is the most straightforward, comprising one chainwheel and a cog that screws directly on to the rear hub. It is the most mechanically efficient set-up as the pedals turn continuously while the bike is in motion. Another advantage is that there is no need for a rear brake; the technique of pushing back on the pedals can be learnt by any experienced cyclist. The disadvantage is that you have to pedal down every hill in a fairly low gear, which cannot be changed when you come to an uphill section of road.

The single freewheel retains some of the advantages of a fixed wheel, but two brakes are required and the introduction of the freewheel mechanism slightly reduces efficiency. This is a useful method of transmission for a beginner as there are no gear levers to worry about. It is also easier to maintain, particularly during the winter when muddy roads and freezing weather can badly compromise the smooth running of variable, derailleur gears.

Hub gears

Being fully enclosed within the enlarged rear hub, these gears are virtually maintenance-free, except for regular lubrication with a light oil. The most common hub gear is the 3-speed. In this, the middle gear is the normal direct drive, like the single freewheel. The higher, and lower, gear ratios are obtained by flicking the handlebar-mounted control lever (or trigger), which activates a system of toothed pinions within the hub. The hub (and consequently the wheel) then turn at a higher speed than the sprocket and chain (and pedals) for a high gear (probably one-third higher than normal); and slower for a low gear (about one-quarter lower than normal).

It is possible to buy hub gears with up to five speeds. Such an arrangement is ideal for small-wheeled bicycles in particular, because you can obtain a good selection of gears without the problems of a derailleur gear operating very close to the road surface.

A disadvantage of the usual 3-speed hub gear is that most beginners find the 'jump' between the middle and top gear to be too high. Therefore, it is advisable to reserve this gear for use downhill, with the wind or along a clear stretch of road when you have time to build up a good pedalling speed. In turn, the low gear should be used for starting off from a stationary position, riding into the wind or uphill. If you still find the hills too steep then you will probably need derailleur gears, which give an almost infinite choice of gear ratios.

Derailleur gears

Derailleur is a French word and simply means 'a mechanism that derails or shifts' the chain from one sprocket to another. The operation of a derailleur is easy to comprehend: you move the control lever (usually fixed to the down tube of the frame) and the cable will shift the gear mechanism, thus moving the chain from one sprocket to another on the 'block' or 'cluster' of sprockets fitted to the rear hub. A second lever may operate a front derailleur to shift the chain between two chainwheels.

Having two chainwheels will double the number of gears available, so the usual arrangement of five sprockets at the back will make a total of 10 gears (the so-called 10-speed bike). A touring bike will sometimes have three chainwheels (to give an extra set of very low gears for touring in hilly terrain), while some racing bikes utilise blocks that have seven sprockets (which require a special chain).

Because of the huge choice of gears offered by a derailleur arrangement, you should never be at a loss for the

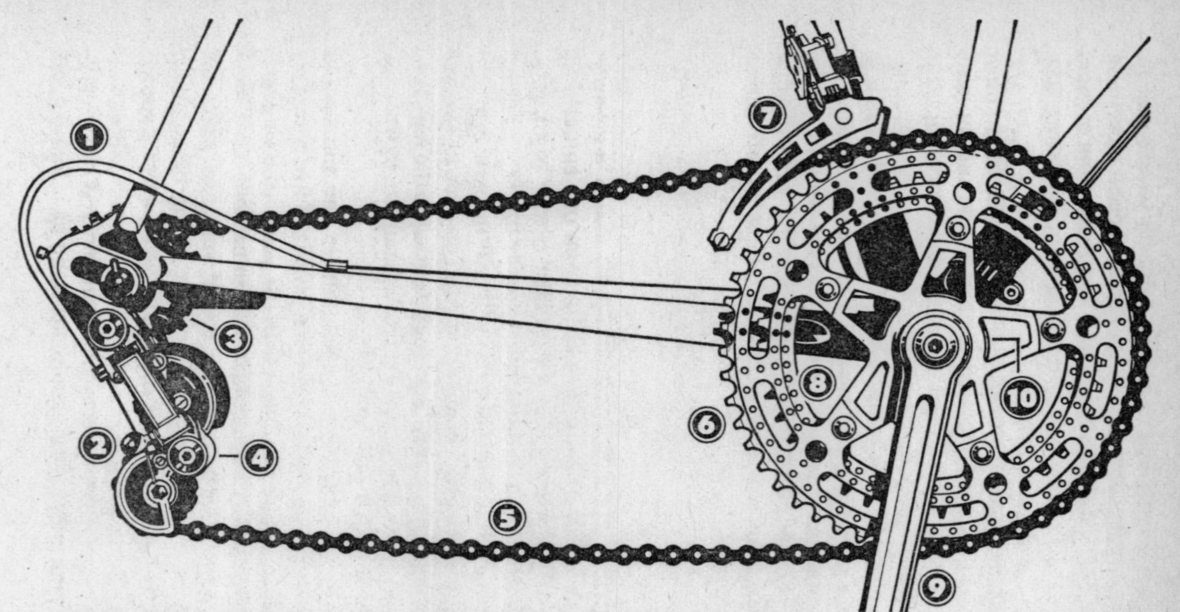

DERAILLEUR GEARS AND TRANSMISSION: 1. Control cable. 2. Lock nut for control cable. 3. Block (or cluster) of five sprockets. 4. Rear derailleur (or changer) mechanism. 5. Chain, 2·4mm wide. 6. Outer chainring – normally has 50–54 teeth. 7. Front derailleur mechanism. 8. Inner chainring – normally has 40–44 teeth. 9. Right-hand crank. 10. Bottom bracket.

Drawing by John Grimwade

correct ratio. However, maintenance is a bigger problem than with hub gears. The usual reason for malfunction is a loose (or even broken) cable, so check weekly that the control cables will move smoothly and that the clamping bolt (or screw) is tight on the gear mechanism itself. Cables stretch with use, so make sure you know how to readjust the gears. The quickest method is to push the lever into the top gear position: if there is any slack in the cable, loosen the rear nut, pull the cable through and retighten the nut.

I often see inexperienced cyclists using derailleur gears as if they were hub gears. That is, they change to the very top gear for most of their riding, and to the very bottom for going up every hill. This is clearly an inefficient method of pedalling, so seek out some advice on using these gears from a more experienced friend, or from the cycle-shop assistant.

If wrongly adjusted, it is possible for the chain to derail completely from the sprockets, perhaps going into the spokes. It is for this reason that some bikes have a large 'spoke protection' disc fitted to the inside of the hub between the sprockets and the spokes. Other bikes have light metal rings around the chainwheels to prevent the chain jumping off at the front. Both of these safety items can give an inexperienced rider more confidence in changing gear, but it is much better to teach them how to keep the gears adjusted correctly, when there should be no danger of the chain jumping off.

Wheels and tyres

Wheels can vary in size from 28-inch diameter down to half that size, but the normal 'big wheel' is 27-inch. It is usual to have 36 spokes in each wheel linking the hub (small or large flange) with the rim (which can be of deep section for roadster-type tyres or of flattish section for racing tyres). To avoid inefficient transfer of the cyclist's pedalling to moving the bike, wheels must be firmly built and as light as practicable. This is because the inertia of the wheel's rolling weight is more difficult to overcome than the dead weight of the frame and other equipment.

It is therefore a wise investment to upgrade a standard production machine with a pair of lighter wheels. For general riding and touring, 'wired on' tyres, which have a separate inner tube, are the best choice. For lightness, rims should be of alloy (not steel) and the tyres should have a narrow section to be fitted to these special rims. For racing or other high-speed riding, tubular tyres are required. These have the inner tube sewn in to the casing, the whole tyre being stuck to the thinner rim by special adhesive. You have to carry a spare tyre with you if using tubulars, but it is a much simpler task to change the complete tyre than it is to locate and mend the puncture of 'wired on' tyres.

The principal advantage of a big-wheel over a small-wheel bike is that the greater circumference will reduce the effect of uneven road surfaces, and the longer spokes will absorb still further the impact of humps and pot-holes. The longer wheelbase of the big-wheel bike will also make it more stable, particularly at low speeds. And, in the long term, big-wheel tyres will not need replacing as often as the smaller variety.

There are a number of different types of valve, which may need different types of pump connections. So make sure that you have the right one for the job. Tyres should be kept inflated correctly, otherwise there is chance of the rubber perishing in the inner tube or on the tread. When not in use, tyres should be kept lightly inflated in a cool, dark environment.

Saddle, handlebars and pedals

There are three areas of contact between the cyclist and the machine: the saddle, handlebars and pedals. Each plays a significant part in the rider's comfort, but it must not be forgotten that for efficient pedalling there should be no sponginess in the system. You should be firmly positioned on the saddle, which acts as a pivot for your legs as well as a means of supporting your weight. Similarly, the handlebars will partly support you as well as acting as a bar on which to pull for added pedalling power. And the pedals must be broad and rigid enough to directly convert your pushing power into turning motion.

A sprung saddle will be uncomfortable for cycling for longer than an hour's duration because you will be bouncing up and down instead of using the whole of your leg movement into turning the pedals. The racing-type saddle is more efficient, but it is essential that your ischial bones (those at the very tops of your legs) sit firmly into the body of the saddle. One that is too narrow to support your particular 'sit bones' will cause unnecessary discomfort, and possible injury. In this respect, it is essential that the saddle is not fitted too high or too far backwards, as in each instance you will tend to slip forward on to the narrower part of the saddle.

There are several types of saddle available. The classic one is made of leather shaped on to a steel wire base: this will prove the most comfortable seat for a cyclist who plans to engage in long-distance touring or racing. Moulded plastic saddles are now more common (and cheaper), the better ones being covered with leather, padded leather or suede. Do not buy a saddle that is too thin as you will experience the same type of bouncing phenomenon as with the sprung saddle. If you are worried about the saddle staining your clothes, it is possible to buy a saddle cover. These are also useful to slip over the saddle to protect it from the elements if the bike has to be left outside at any time.

The choice of handlebars is very much a personal choice, but avoid those which have excessive width (such as high-risers) or are excessively deep (these are designed for track sprinting). Straight ’bars are adequate for town riding or other short-distance cycling, but they offer only one position to grip. If used for longer journeys, you will almost certainly develop aches in back, shoulders and arms from this limited arrangement. This is why so-called drop handlebars are recommended for more serious cycling. These handlebars can be gripped in three basic positions: on the ‘drops’ for going fast downhill or riding into the wind; on the tops for pulling yourself up hills, holding the straight centre section; or on the brake hoods, which is the most comfortable, normal position.

Pedals come in three basic types: double-sided with rubber bars; so-called rat-trap pedals, also double-sided; and platform pedals, for use with toe clips and straps. The rubber protected pedals are designed so that you can use normal walking shoes without getting unpleasant marks on the soles. The metal rat-trap pedals can be used with or without toe clips. They will give a firmer base for pedalling and your foot will be less liable to slip off. The use of toe clips is recommended as they will help guide your foot into the right place on the pedal (ball of the foot over the pedal axle). It is a common fear that you will get your foot trapped in the toe clip when you have to stop suddenly, but there is no need to tighten the toe straps and you will find that you will soon become adept at ‘picking up’ the pedals when on the move.

Brakes

Nearly every bike is equipped with some form of rim brake, although it is possible to buy a hub brake when extra braking is required (on a tandem for instance), while many American machines have back-pedalling coaster brakes. Research is still being done into the development of disc brakes, which could ultimately prove more efficient. Rim brakes lose much of their efficiency on wet roads, so it is important to start braking earlier in the wet so the rims have a chance to dry out before full braking pressure is applied.

Rim brakes can be operated by metal rods (which are heavy and rather cumbersome) or by cables (lighter and more efficient, there being a direct link between lever and brake). There are three designs of caliper (or scissor-type) brakes: side pull, centre pull (both of which are fixed to the frame above the forks) and brazed on (which operate on the centre-pull system, but each arm of the brake is brazed to a special boss on the fork legs).

Each type of brake has its particular drawbacks, a fact which makes maintenance essential. Replace brake blocks that are worn, make regular checks that the rims are gripped by the blocks along their whole length and keep the cables running smoothly, with no slackness. These are simple precautions, but can mean the difference between stopping safely and having a crash.

What type of bike?

Different shapes and sizes of frame can be equipped with virtually any combination of the components detailed above. I have had extensive experience of riding each different type (see illustrations in Appendix Two). Small-wheeled machines are useful for short-distance riding in towns, being ideal for shopping, the low centre of gravity remaining when a loaded bag (or basket) is fitted to a carrier fixed over the rear wheel. But I have found that general riding and touring is much easier on a traditional diamond frame with large wheels.

A beginner should start with a bike in the medium price range, preferably a production model from a reputable manufacturer and bought from a recognised cycle dealer. You will then have a bicycle that has proven components and one that has been checked over properly. Bearing in mind what I have said before and particularly if money is a prime consideration, then look for a good second-hand lightweight rather than spend the same amount on a new heavyweight.

Cycling should be enjoyable, and you will never get fit if you are discouraged by the exercise being too hard.

CHAPTER SEVEN

It Takes Two to Tandem

Having a family is no deterrent to maintaining a regular programme of cyling. Babies can safely be transported by bicycle from about 15 months old, an age at which they are strong enough to sit upright for extended periods – although more than an hour at a stretch is not recommended. There are many different types of baby seat on the market, including the type pictured on the front cover of this book. This is rear mounted, the safest arrangement, giving the child the greatest protection from the wind.

The baby is strapped firmly into the seat, which has a rigid metal framework that should be bolted on to the frame of the bicycle or tandem. Our daughter was using one of these seats until she was five years old, when she started to outgrow it, her legs starting to become cramped. She did not like travelling in cold weather too much, probably because she was stationary and not pedalling, and therefore not maintaining her body heat with exercise. And my wife was not too keen on being poked in the back from timc to time, or being assaulted with a constant stream of questions from the inquisitive infant behind!

It is possible to buy seats that fix to the top tube of the bike frame, in front of the cyclist. This is a dangerous arrangement, as the centre of gravity of the bike is raised and the baby would be thrown forward in the event of a sudden stop or crash. An alternative, if rather cumbersome, method is to fix a sidecar or trailer to the bike. This has the advantage of giving the baby a comfortable environment, but the low position means that there is very restricted vision for the child.

In the rear seat, a baby has plenty to look at, to hear and

to smell. All these experiences will enhance its awareness and knowledge of the world outside the home, which can only be of benefit to its education. It will also give young children an awareness of traffic conditions, which will help them in gaining confidence when it comes to cycling themselves on the roads.

Our daughter had her first two-wheeler bike (with stabilisers) shortly after her third birthday, and was riding it without stabilisers when she was 3½ years old. If a child is introduced to cycling at this age, they will be confident enough to ride on the road before they are six, accompanied of course by a parent or responsible teenager. Emma was riding a bicycle with larger wheels, with freewheel and brakes, shortly after her fifth birthday.

They will not be able to attain a normal adult speed, or maintain it, until they are older than seven years. The in-between stage can be covered by fixing special pedals to the rear of a tandem so that the child can operate them from the rear saddle position. The pedal arrangement clamps to the seat tube of the frame and the child's pedals turn a chain that engages with the normal rear chainwheel of the tandem.

Progress will be rapid as a child grows, and (as mentioned earlier) an eight-year-old has ridden the 3,000-miles coast-to-coast trail with his family across the United States. By the time a child is 10 or 11 years, they should be trusted to ride alone on the road, or with friends their own age. Before this is sanctioned, it is recommended that they are put through the excellent Cycling Proficiency Scheme, organised in Britain by RoSPA. They will be taught roadcraft, hand signals and how to recognise road signs; and then have to pass a test that is normally conducted by police officers.

Some children will develop sufficient independence before 10 years, and you may have read the experience of (now veteran) cyclist Harry Keates in the photographic section of this book. He was eight years old when he undertook a

100 miles ride on his own (from Oxford to London and back). His example shows that cycling is an exercise that will benefit children in terms of fitness, health and adventure.

There are numerous opportunities for pupils at secondary schools to take part in organised cycling events. School cycling clubs have been established under the auspices of the English Schools Cycling Association (ESCA), a body run by an enthusiastic band of cycling-minded teachers. Club rides, touring and all phases of cycle racing are catered for by ESCA, that organises annual area and national championships in various age groups. Because of its efforts, cycling has become an alternative games subject on many school curricula.

Cycling is also being promoted as a sport at various centres in Great Britain. In the London area, for instance, professional coaches conduct training sessions for school groups at The Eastway road racing circuit in the Lea Valley Regional Park; at Herne Hill Stadium in South London; and at the cycling track in Paddington Recreation Ground, West London.

Regular cycling competition is available in events held under the control of the British Cycling Federation (track and road racing), the Road Time Trials Council (time trials) and the British Cyclo-Cross Association (cyclo-cross). To take part in these sectors of the sport it is best to become a member of a local cycling club – ask at your library, or contact one of the above bodies (addresses in Appendix Six).

For those wanting to sample more serious cycling, but without the expense of acquiring a racing bike, there are a number of alternatives. The Cyclists' Touring Club (CTC) organise invitation rides at regular intervals; these are open to adults as well as schoolchildren. Various organised tours are run by the Youth Hostels Association (YHA). Individuals can enter the Duke of Edinburgh's award scheme with cycling as the nominated discipline. And the

Viking Schools Challenge, started in 1978, gives children in the under-15 and under-13 age groups the chance to participate in events at their own school before qualifying for regional and national finals.

Riding a bike to school every day is probably the best way in which teenagers can keep fit, while giving them a sense of independence. It is also one of the quickest means of travelling to school. When I first started at secondary school, I used the bus, which involved a long walk at the other end. It was usually a half-hour trip from door-to-door. Later, I decided that it would be just as quick to walk (it was) and I pocketed the bus fares. Eventually, I progressed to cycling to school and the time for the two-mile journey was cut to 10 minutes.

For parents who are not keen to spend a large sum of money on buying their offspring a 5- or 10-speed lightweight, I have this advice. Look on it as an investment. A well-built bicycle will give their child years of service before it is outgrown; and then it can be sold second-hand and replaced by a larger model. It will give independence to the child, who could well become interested in day trips with their friends and then progress to holidays on the bike.

Cycle touring holidays are generally inexpensive, thereby saving you the outlay of including the child on a foreign package holiday. Or, if you take motoring holidays, why not take the kids' bikes on the roof rack so that they will have their own means of transport at your destination. In these ways, a new (and well used) bicycle will quickly pay for itself.

There are an increasing number of tandems being marketed today, some of the best coming from France, where touring models are produced by large manufacturers such as Peugeot, Gitane and Lejeune. These machines make much use of lightweight alloy components and are comparable in weight and performance to tandems custom-built by lightweight manufacturers that are many times more expensive. It is also possible to buy second-hand tandems that may have survived from the 1930s, a period when tandem riding was at its peak in Britain.

Tandem riding is a superb method of combining the efforts of two people who may be unevenly matched on two single bicycles. Touring can become tiresome if one rider is constantly dropping behind, or vice versa. But with parent and child, husband and wife, boyfriend and girlfriend or brother and sister riding together on a tandem, they can share the same experiences and physical efforts. There is always someone to talk with.

There are snags of course. The extra weight can make hill climbing a difficult task unless you have some very low gears to use. And, downhill, you will probably need extra braking. This could be special tandem caliper brakes (which have longer brake blocks than standard) or a hub brake (which will be part of the rear hub). Even then it is still possible to have problems on long descents when overheating of rims or brake shoes could occur.

Learning to ride a tandem is best done on a road that goes downhill because the most difficult part is co-ordinating the starting efforts of the two riders. Learn how to freewheel at first, before going on to actual pedalling. Do not worry about some initial wobbles, they will soon smooth out once you can build up a little speed. A more difficult problem can be turning corners. The rider at the back, if experienced at normal cycling, may tend to steer (or try to), which results in the frame being subjected to an unusual side pressure.

It can also be difficult to properly co-ordinate each rider's efforts when changing gear or braking or starting to freewheel. Before such liaison becomes automatic, the one in front should state clearly each time a change of gear is imminent, or when the brakes are to be applied. The front rider should also say when a change of direction is coming up – the one at the back (the 'stoker') can then make the necessary hand signal.

Starting from scratch, the first tandem ride I took with

my wife was twice round the block. Having decided we liked it (we were borrowing a friend's tandem), we next went for an afternoon ride of about 25 miles on a fairly flat route into the countryside. It was an exhilarating experience pedalling smoothly along on the flat at 25–30 mph. The impetus of a second pair of legs gave an unusual sense of added power.

Since buying our own tandem (see front cover), we have covered up to 100 miles in a day on weekend rides. We have rarely experienced any dangerous moments, finding that traffic tends to give a tandem a much wider berth than it does a bicycle. This is especially true when Emma is sitting in the child seat at the rear, perhaps making the hand signals!

Tandems can be ridden by couples of any age or differing size. I have seen a tandem pair of well over pension age on the top of the 8,000 ft Great St Bernard Pass in Switzerland, looking quite happy with life. And I know of another couple who ride thousands of miles on their tandem, although the husband is well over 6 ft tall and the wife less than 5 ft.

The key to good tandem riding is relaxation, something which comes naturally the more cycling you do. But it is just one of the many enjoyable facets of this unique means of transport: the bicycle. Use it to enhance your life.

Cycling could improve your breathing, your health and your fitness. So dig that old bike out of the garage or start studying the classified columns of your local paper, today. And start pedalling. It is never too late.

APPENDIX ONE

A to Z of Problems (and prevention)

Accidents

In Great Britain, between 20,000 and 25,000 cyclists were involved in accidents each year from 1975 to 1978. About 20 per cent of the accidents resulted in serious injuries or death. The largest proportion of accidents (about 40 per cent) happened to 10–16 year olds, which underlines the importance of teaching children to learn cycling techniques and road sense before they reach the age of 10. Surveys show that the safest roads to use are secondary roads and lanes in country areas – these are also the most pleasant routes. Members of the Cyclists Touring Club and the British Cycling Federation are covered for third party insurance and receive legal aid in case of accidents. It is also advisable to take out personal accident insurance.

Bonk

In cyclists' terminology, bonk (or hunger knock) is the feeling of great fatigue experienced during a long ride if you have neglected to eat enough food during the ride. The warning signs are weakness, dizziness, possibly nausea and drowsiness. Cure is to stop and eat some instant energy food (e.g. fruit, fruit bars, glucose-type energy drinks). Prevention is to nibble at a little food every few miles during a long ride.

Cramp

Cyclists are often liable to cramp in thigh and calf muscles in hot weather. Dehydration is the probable cause, so drink at regular intervals during longer rides, but not too much at a time. Plastic bottles can be fitted into specially made 'cages' that fit to down tube of bike, or on to handlebars. Avoid sticky drinks. Mineral water is good or one of the patent athletic drinks. It is also possible to get cramp in feet and toes if you use tightly fitting or soft-soled shoes.

Dogs

Loose dogs can cause a serious nuisance to cyclists, particularly in rural areas of Europe, North America and elsewhere. Dogs have been known to run into cyclists and cause a crash, which is particularly dangerous if the animal runs out unexpectedly. Large dogs could jump up at a cyclist and inflict bite wounds or rip clothing. One answer is to get up speed when approaching a dog that looks likely to chase you and to shout at it very loudly when alongside. If this does not scare it off, continue sprinting until it gives up the chase. It is also possible to buy patent dog-scarers, such as a spray that will cause the dog's eyes to water. Another available 'weapon', as a last resort, is your bicycle pump.

Eyes

Damage to eyes by wind-blown grit, flies or bright sunshine is possible. Some cyclists suffer from conjunctivitis as a result. Visit your doctor if you have any such problems. To minimise the nuisance, wear sun glasses in sunny weather, or even ski-type goggles. A peaked cap or cycling hat will protect the eyes from dazzling sunshine and will also stop most flies and pieces of grit from striking your face. If you use embrocation on leg muscles, make sure that your hands are washed clean afterwards. It is quite possible for embrocation to cause irritation to the eyes.

Freezing weather

Icy roads put cyclists in immediate danger, particularly on bends and on downhill stretches. A prevention is to let some air from your tyres, which should have thick treads for winter cycling. Derailleur gear mechanisms or cables could get frozen, so try to prevent this by changing gear at frequent intervals. To ease the effects of a tumble, and to keep warm, wear at least two layers of clothing (including socks). Wool is the best material underneath.

Gears

Badly maintained gear control cables, or wrongly adjusted gear mechanisms, will seriously hamper the smooth operation of gears. Check these items weekly and insert a little light oil into cable casing where possible and on to gear lever. Keep all lock nuts (or bolts) firmly tightened. If a cable snaps during a ride, screw the rear derailleur stop nut until the chain engages with a middle sprocket (not the smallest one).

Horses

Moving cyclists, particularly in a group, will often panic a horse. Therefore, slow down when approaching horses on the road and give them some warning of your approach. And give the horses a wide berth when you pass in case the animal decides to rear or kick.

Itineraries

Choosing the best itinerary for any cycle ride is a significant problem, even for an experienced cyclist. For touring, it is possible to apply to the CTC, YHA or BCF for advice; specific route details are available for most popular areas. For short trips, use a large-scale map (Ordnance Survey

1 : 50,000 is ideal) to seek alternatives to main roads. For longer journeys, use the 1 : 100,000 scale that covers Britain. For the Continent, several road maps at the 1 : 200,000 scale are produced (e.g. the Michelin series for France, Belgium and Switzerland). It is generally advisable to choose an itinerary that uses winding side roads rather than straight, major roads.

Jarring

Cobbles, unmade surfaces or badly maintained roads can cause uncomfortable jarring to a cyclist's hands, arms and seat. The answer is to keep the elbows bent, with your hands resting lightly on the bars (or brake-lever hoods), so that forces are not directed straight into the body. Lift your seat off the saddle if you can see an unavoidable hump or pot-hole in the road.

Knees

Aching knees are one of the most common complaints from cyclists. The cause could be mechanical – bent crank, bent pedal or over use of high gears – resulting in uneven pressure on the knee joints; or physical – cold weather for instance. Simple measures that can be taken are to keep knees covered (except in hot weather), to warm up properly before making hard efforts, and to apply a warming embrocation to area of skin covering knee before riding in very cold conditions.

Luggage

Carrying bulky or heavy items can be a major problem. For shopping, the answer can be a wire basket mounted on a rear baggage support, a wicker basket fixed to the handlebars or a shoulder bag (or rucksack). For longer trips and touring, a saddlebag is recommended. When greater capacity is needed (long tours, cycle camping, etc.), the load can be more evenly distributed by using panniers (either mounted on a front or rear carrier) in combination with a saddlebag. Small items (and food) are best kept handy in a small handlebar-mounted bag.

Motor vehicles

The majority of accidents involving both bicycles and motor vehicles are caused by motorists. This can be through opening of car doors into the path of a cyclist (so give parked cars a wide berth); a car turning left in front of a cyclist on the inside (look for signs of a car turning and stay behind if you are on inside); a car turning right into the path of a cyclist travelling in the opposite direction (keep a look out for vehicles at junctions and ride cautiously); or a vehicle cutting in front of a cyclist too soon after overtaking (keep alert to any such manoeuvre and always think ahead to plan evasive action).

Nails

To avoid the risk of punctures, keep a constant lookout for nails, grit or any other objects that may be on the road surface, and steer clear of them. It is also good policy to not ride too close to the gutter. Tyre savers (or flint catchers) are specially made loops of plastic-coated wire that fit to the brake bolt and rest lightly on the tyre, removing any objects from the tread as the wheel turns.

Oil

Lack of oil on chains, in hubs and in bottom brackets could cause the transmission to seize up. Regular lubrication of these parts is essential, but excess oil is also to be avoided. An over-oiled chain will attract grit and thus cause unnecessary wear to chainrings and cogs.

Punctures

Make a quick check of your tyres for cuts or grit in the tread before every trip. Ensure that valves do not stick out from the rim at an angle. And always keep tyres properly inflated. These three precautions will greatly reduce the likelihood of puncturing. If you do have to repair a puncture, make sure that you have the necessary repair outfit before starting the ride, and never rush the repair. Stick the patch carefully over the puncture in the tube and dust with french chalk, if you have an inner tube and wired-on tyre. For riders with racing (tubular) tyres, always carry at least one spare tyre, preferably two. Spare tyres should be stored on a rim, lightly inflated, not folded up.

Quick-release

Racing bikes have quick-release levers to fix the hubs to frame and many small-wheel bikes have quick-release levers to adjust saddle and handlebar heights. Check before every ride that the levers are adjusted correctly, not over-tight or at all loose. The hub quick-release levers should point in towards the frame so as not to make a dangerous projection.

Rain

Besides causing problems for the rider (how do you keep dry?), rain can create serious trouble for the bicycle. In the August 1978 *Which?* report, it was shown that wet roads can increase the stopping distance of some bicycles to 160 ft (50 metres), a fact which emphasises the need to keep your distance behind other vehicles on the road. It is possible to buy special wet-weather brake blocks, which will improve brake performance, but great care in the wet is the best policy. After riding in the wet, use a cloth to dry off water from any steel parts to discourage rust formation. Water can also get into ball races (in bottom bracket, hubs, pedals and headset). The only proper cure for this is to dismantle the parts (unless there are sealed-bearing units, when the problem does not arise), dry them out and reassemble with new grease. The best prevention is to make an overhaul (once or twice a year), checking for wear in ball races and ensuring there is sufficient grease to keep out water.

Snow

It is unpleasant riding a bike through thick snow when it is falling, but it is possible to ride a bike on snowy roads, unless it is very deep. Hard-packed snow is a more difficult surface to negotiate than loose snow. So do not be put off from riding your bike with snow on the ground. There is a club in North America that boasts a sub-zero badge, awarded to members who ride a distance of 50 miles in a day when the air temperature does not average more than zero degrees Farenheit!

Theft

About 20,000 bikes were stolen in the London area during 1977, so theft can be a real problem, especially in urban areas. To protect your bike when it is parked, use a reputable padlock and chain to fix the bike to iron railings or a lamp post (unless you can take the bike indoors). If you have quick-release wheels, take the front one out and put chain through this, the frame and the rear wheel, and lock to the railings. Remove the pump and bag, taking them with you. To aid recovery of a bike if it is stolen, report the theft immediately to the police. To assist them, it is important that you have a full description of the bike (a photograph if possible) and a note of the frame number (this will probably be marked on the bottom bracket). Another precaution is to insure the bicycle against theft – ask at the bike shop where you buy your bike.

Urban traffic

Rush-hour traffic in towns can be a deterrent to inexperienced cyclists. Avoid it if possible by seeking out quiet back-street routes, perhaps utilising short stretches of carriageways where cars are banned (e.g. park roads, towpaths, cycleways) and making maximum use of bus lanes (which cyclists can use, except for contra-flow routes). In urban traffic, overtake stationary queues of traffic on the outside because a car door could open on the inside lane. Give firm hand signals and move in plenty of time if you wish to turn right, constantly checking the traffic movements behind and in front of you.

Vitamins

Lack of vitamins or minerals can be a problem for cyclists who ride regularly long distances. Prevention is to increase the proportion of fresh (raw) fruit and vegetables in the diet, perhaps supplementing this with vitamin C tablets (100 grammes or more) and multi-vitamin tablets.

Wheels

Special attention should be given to the upkeep of the wheels. Replace spokes that break, and keep tension in spokes by regular checks. File down spoke ends from rim before fitting a new tyre or tube. Take wheels out to clean hub, spokes and rims at least once a week. Corrosion can soon eat into spokes.

X–Y–Z

The last word on problems is to remember that prevention is better than cure. This applies to both the bicycle and the body. Most problems need never occur if this advice is taken. Practice balancing before learning to ride. And learn how to ride properly before undertaking an exercise programme. This book has hopefully put you on the right guidelines to using cycling as a means of transport and as a passport to fitness. The bicycle is one of the most perfect machines ever invented – make enjoyable use of it.

APPENDIX TWO

Buying – Points to Check

<table>
<tr><th></th><th>NEW BIKE</th><th>USED BIKE</th></tr>
<tr><td>Frame</td><td colspan="2">Size (measured from centre of bottom bracket to top of seat tube) should be about 11 inches (280 mm) less than rider's inside leg measurement (from crotch to floor). Check frame's alignment: looking from the back, both wheels should turn in the same vertical plane.</td></tr>
<tr><td></td><td>Apply front brake and push bike forward to check tightness of head-set.</td><td>Lift front end and turn handle-bars to check for any pitting of ball bearings in headset. Check tightness of bolt clamping seat pin into frame. Look for any signs of rust at tube/lug joints and at bottom bracket.</td></tr>
<tr><td>Cranks</td><td colspan="2">Hold cranks at pedals and exert pressure at right angles to frame to check for looseness in bottom bracket assembly. Lift rear end, turn pedals and check for any play (wobbling) in chain rings – rings may need fixing tightly or actual crank could be bent.</td></tr>
<tr><td></td><td></td><td>With rear brake applied, check for looseness in cotter pins (or axle bolts, if cotterless) by applying pressure to cranks in plane parallel to chain. Check steel cranks for signs of rust.</td></tr>
<tr><td>Pedals</td><td colspan="2">Put foot on pedal to ensure that it is wide enough for your foot. Check that pedal is fitted squarely and tightly into crank (if possible, use a pedal spanner to unscrew pedal, then re-tighten).</td></tr>
<tr><td></td><td></td><td>Turn pedals on axles to check for any tightness. Check that frame of pedal is not loose or rusty. Undo dust-cap to check for grit or rust on axle nut.</td></tr>
<tr><td>Saddle</td><td colspan="2">Check that saddle clip (or bolts) are tight. Sit on saddle to make sure that it is broad enough to support your 'sit bones', but not too wide to make pedalling uncomfortable.</td></tr>
</table>

<table>
<tr><th></th><th>NEW BIKE</th><th>USED BIKE</th></tr>
<tr><td></td><td>Look from rear to check that point of saddle is in line with top tube of frame. Ask if new leather saddle has been treated or not.</td><td>Check that saddle has not sagged (if leather one) or has not become deformed (check springs on sprung saddle).</td></tr>
<tr><td>Wheels</td><td colspan="2">Spin wheels individually to check for trueness (there may be a broken or missing spoke in an old wheel) and smoothness (over-tightened hub cones or pitted ball races will cause stickiness). Check that wheels are fixed tightly into frame before test riding it.</td></tr>
<tr><td></td><td>Before use, remove any grease from rim, otherwise brakes will not function properly.</td><td>Check for loose spokes, dents in rim and rust.</td></tr>
<tr><td>Tyres</td><td colspan="2">If soft, inflate to check that valves function correctly and that there are no leaks. Racing (tubular) tyres should be stuck firmly to rim, and should be bedded evenly.</td></tr>
<tr><td></td><td>Check that tread is aligned and fixed firmly to tyre fabric.</td><td>Check for lack of tread, bulges and cuts in fabric. Valves should be at right angles to rims, with locating nut for each where applicable.</td></tr>
<tr><td>Brakes</td><td colspan="2">Check that brake blocks are adjusted to engage with rims along their full length. Cables should move smoothly within plastic cover. Cable lock nuts should be tight.</td></tr>
<tr><td></td><td>Check that you can operate levers with hands in normal riding position. Check that cables are fitted firmly to bicycle frame.</td><td>Check for badly worn brake blocks, frayed cables and loose brake levers. To check efficiently push bike forward with front brake applied, backwards with rear brake applied.</td></tr>
<tr><td>Handlebars</td><td colspan="2">Make sure that handlebars are not too wide or too far from saddle by sitting on bike and placing hands in riding position. Plugs should be firmly fixed into handlebar ends.</td></tr>
<tr><td></td><td></td><td>Check that stem bolt is clamped firmly, with no signs of cracks or bad rusting.</td></tr>
<tr><td>Chain</td><td>New chain should not be stretched or too loose. For bikes with hub gear or one sprocket, there should be about ½ inch (13 mm) of play at mid-point of chain.</td><td>If chain is badly stretched, it will noticeably 'droop'. If so, both chain and rear sprockets will have to be renewed. Check for stiff chain links – there could be rust underneath a film of oil.</td></tr>
</table>

SMALL WHEEL
(3-speed)

Suitable for shopping or about town cycling. Low price range. Model shown is folding version, with quick-release levers for frame, saddle height and handlebars. Has cottered chainset and single freewheel gear. Can be bought with hub gear, giving 3-speed. Has sprung saddle and rubber-sided pedals.

JUVENILE SPORTS
(10-speed)

Most popular type for teenagers. Medium price range. Model shown has cottered chainset, rat-trap pedals, 10-speed derailleur gears, chainwheel protector, centre-pull brakes and full mudguards. Has long wheelbase, to cater for mudguards, and high-pressure tyres.

LADIES' TOURER
(10-speed)

For women wanting to ride bike in dress or skirt. Medium price range. This model has 10-speed derailleur gears, with low bottom gear; chainwheel protector; quilted plastic saddle; full mudguards; high-pressure tyres; side-pull brakes; and rubber-sided pedals.

MEN'S COMMUTER
(5-speed)

Useful commuting bike. Medium price range. Cottered cranks, chainring protector, spoke protector disc, handlebar-mounted gear lever, 5-speed derailleur gear, straight handlebars, rear luggage support, high-pressure tyres and rubber-sided pedals.

TOURING SPECIAL
(5-speed)

More sophisticated versions are available, with cotterless chainsets and fully equipped with panniers and bags. This model in medium price range. Has 5-speed derailleur gears, full plastic mudguards, leather saddle, rat-trap pedals, high-pressure tyres and rubber-hooded brake levers.

RACING LIGHTWEIGHT
(12-speed)

Special lightweight frame and equipment. High price range. Short chain-stays, giving close clearance to rear wheel. Cotterless chainset. Six sprockets at rear, two chainrings to give 12-speed derailleur gears. Has quick-release racing wheels and tubular tyres. Rubber-hooded brake levers and leather saddle.

Drawings by John Grimwade

	NEW BIKE	USED BIKE
Gears (hub)	If possible, ride bike to check that all the gears can be engaged without slipping, that changes are smooth and that 'trigger' can be operated without stretching. Check that gear lever is clamped firmly to bike and that cable runs smoothly.	
Gears (derailleur)	Lift bike at back, turn pedals and check that chain will 'derail' on to each rear sprocket – and will not overshoot at either side. Make similar check for chainwheel derailleur, if fitted. Check that gear levers are fixed firmly to frame and that there is no 'sponginess' in operation of levers. All cables should be lightly greased to ensure smooth operation.	Check cables for fraying or kinks. Test gear mechanism for looseness at joints.
Accessories	Mudguards should not touch tyres when wheels are spun. Mudguard stays should not protrude dangerously. Pump should fit firmly to the frame and should function efficiently. When pedals are turned, there must be no overlap between toe clips (or foot) and front wheel (or mudguard). Lights must be of correct British standard, must function correctly and must fix firmly to the bike.	
General	Before buying, ask for a short test ride so that you can check for any unusual noises coming from the pedals, cranks, bottom bracket, chain or hubs. Also check that, when pedalling, the fronts of your shoes do not touch or overlap the front wheel (or mudguard); the result would be a crash if this happened on turning a sharp corner. Ask for a tool kit, puncture repair outfit and a reputable cycle lock. And when buying from a dealer, find out if the manufacturer offers free insurance or a long guarantee.	

APPENDIX THREE

Gear Sizes

Gear sizes in Britain and North America are still quoted on the traditional inch system. In the text, a gear of 70 inches is quoted as being a medium-sized gear. This 70 inches is what the equivalent wheel size (diameter) would have been on a 'penny-farthing' bicycle. To give this figure some meaning you have to calculate the equivalent circumference of the penny-farthing wheel (i.e. multiply 70 by 'pi' = 220·8 inches = 18·4 feet). Therefore, for every complete turn of the pedals on a 70-inch gear, the bike moves forward a little more than six yards.

The Continental system of gear sizes (expressed in metres) is based on the actual distance moved forward for one pedal revolution. So the 70-inch gear would become a gear of 5·6 metres (18·4 ft = 5·6 m).

Gear tables are a handy means of checking the gear size for each combination of chainrings and sprockets. The following table is for the standard wheel size of 27 inches diameter. To understand the table, the quoted 70-inch gear could be obtained by using a 44-teeth chainring with a 17-teeth sprocket (actually 69·9 inches). To convert these inch gear sizes to the metric Continental system, divide by 100 and multiply by 8 (e.g. 70 × 0·08 = 5·6 m).

GEAR TABLE (for 27-inch wheels)

Chain wheel ⇨	38	40	42	44	46	47	48	49	50	51	52	53
Sprocket ⇩												
12	85·5	90·0	94·5	99·0	103·5	105·7	108·0	110·2	112·5	114·7	117·0	119·3
13	78·9	83·1	87·2	91·4	95·5	97·6	99·7	101·8	103·9	105·9	108·0	110·1
14	73·3	77·1	81·0	84·9	88·7	90·6	92·6	94·5	96·4	98·3	100·3	102·2
15	68·4	72·0	75·6	79·2	82·8	84·6	86·4	88·2	90·0	91·8	93·6	95·4
16	64·1	67·5	70·9	74·3	77·6	79·3	81·0	82·7	84·4	86·1	87·8	89·4
17	60·3	63·5	66·7	69·9	73·1	74·6	76·2	77·8	79·4	81·0	82·6	84·1
18	57·0	60·0	63·0	66·0	69·0	70·5	72·0	73·5	75·0	76·5	78·0	79·5
19	54·0	56·8	59·7	62·5	65·4	66·8	68·2	69·6	71·1	72·5	73·9	75·3
20	51·3	54·0	56·7	59·4	62·1	63·4	64·8	66·2	67·5	68·8	70·2	71·5
21	48·9	51·4	54·0	56·6	59·1	60·4	61·7	63·0	64·3	65·6	66·9	68·1
22	46·6	49·1	51·5	54·0	56·5	57·7	58·9	60·1	61·4	62·5	63·8	65·0
23	44·6	47·0	49·3	51·6	54·0	55·2	56·3	57·5	58·7	59·8	61·0	62·2
24	42·8	45·0	47·3	49·5	51·8	52·9	54·0	55·1	56·2	57·3	58·5	59·6
25	41·0	43·2	45·4	47·5	49·7	50·8	51·8	52·9	54·0	55·1	56·2	57·2
26	39·5	41·5	43·6	45·7	47·8	48·8	49·9	50·9	51·9	53·0	54·0	55·0
28	36·6	38·6	40·5	42·4	44·4	45·3	46·3	47·2	48·2	49·1	50·1	51·1

APPENDIX FOUR

Bicycle Brand Names (and manufacturers)

BRITISH MANUFACTURED BICYCLES

Allegro Cycles (Pleasant Street, West Bromwich). Economically priced ranges of sports bikes (Formula One and Super Star) and small-wheelers (Top Twenty).

Barelli (Viking Way, Bar Hill, Cambridge). Lightweight frames manufactured, as well as other equipment.

Bickerton Cycles Vulcan Lighting & Leisure (Moorsome Street, Birmingham). Conventional bikes manufactured as well as famed Bickerton folding, lightweight, small-wheeler.

Bromwich Cycles (Far Gosford Street, Coventry). Small manufacturer of lightweight bikes and frames.

Brown Brothers (Stratton St Margaret, Swindon, Wilts). Manufacturer of Vindec bicycles; and importers of Zizi pavement cycles.

Carlton Cycles (Kilton Road, Worksop, Notts). Manufacturer of Carlton lightweight and sports bikes. Branch of TI Raleigh.

Chessington Cycles (Oakcroft Road, Chessington, Surrey). Manufacturer of Chessington range of sports bikes and small-wheelers; importer of Soma and Maruishi bikes from Japan.

Condor Cycles (Grays Inn Road, London WC1). Manufacturer of custom built cycles for racing or touring.

Crown Cycles (Baltimore Road, Perry Bar, Birmingham). Manufacturer of Crown Lightweight bikes.

Dawes Cycles (Wharf Road, Tyseley, Birmingham). Manufacturer of sports and lightweight bikes.

Elswick-Hopper Cycles (Barton-upon-Humber, South Humberside). Manufacturer of range of Cosmopolitan family bikes and Elswick sports bikes.

F. W. Evans Cycles (The Cut, London SE1). Maker of specialist racing and touring tricycles.

Falcon Cycles (Marsh Lane, Barton-upon-Humber). Manufacturer of Falcon lightweights, Coventry Eagle sports and family bikes; concessionary manufacturer of Eddy Merckx sports bikes.

Halfords (Washford West, Redditch, Worcs). Through own retail stores, sells its manufactured range of Halfords sports bikes and small-wheelers.

Holdsworthy Co (Oakfield Road, London SE 20). Manufacturer of Holdsworth racing bikes, Claud Butler lightweights and Freddie Grubb lightweights.

JRJ Cycles (Harehills Lane, Leeds). Manufacturer of Bob Jackson and Merlin racing lightweights and Bob Jackson tandems.

Ron Kitching (Hookstone Park, Harrogate). Manufacturer of Ron Kitching lightweight bikes; importer of vast range of equipment and accessories.

Mercian Cycles (Ascot Drive, Derby). Manufacturer of specialist racing and lightweight bikes and tandems.

Micro Cycles (Station Road, Coleshill, Birmingham). Manufacturer of folding small-wheelers and small-wheel tandems.

MKM Cycles (Skipton Road, Harrogate). Small manufacturer of lightweight and racing bikes.

Moorland Cycles (Lily Street, Milnrow, Rochdale). Manufacturer of Moorland range of small-wheelers and sports bikes; importer of French Gitane sports bikes and tandems.

Pashley Cycles (Masons Road, Stratford-upon-Avon). Manufacturer of Piccolo small-wheeler and traditional big-wheel bikes, tandems and tricycles.

Harry Quinn Cycles (Walton Road, Liverpool). Specialist manufacturer of racing and lightweight bikes.

TI Raleigh Industries (Lenton Boulevard, Nottingham). World's largest manufacturer of bicycles, including TI Raleigh racing and lightweight bikes, sports models, small-wheelers and fun bikes.

Trusty Manufacturing Co (Cranborne Road, Potters Bar, Herts). Manufacturer of Viscount range of sports and lightweight bikes.

Viking Cycles (Kingsland Grange Industrial Estate, Warrington, Lancs). Factory in Northern Ireland produces quality range of lightweight, sports and racing bikes.

IMPORTED BICYCLES

Mark Abrahams & Sons (Gordon Road, Waltham Abbey, Essex). Importers of Kalkhoff sports, touring and junior bicycles from West Germany.

Anglo Foreign Trading (Featherstone Street, London EC1). Importers of Pannonia range of children's small-wheelers and sports bikes.

Arrow Bicycle Co (18 Constitution Hill, Leicester). Italian racing bikes and full range of sports and small-wheel bikes imported.

J. L. Attias (Millmead, Guildford, Surrey). Italian-made range of racing, touring and small-wheel bikes.

Capital Trading Co (Great Sutton Street, London EC1). Mayfair and Chelsea small-wheelers, Cadillac fun bikes imported.

Caratti Sport (Chelford Grove, Patchway, Bristol). Importer of Italian Benotto racing bikes and Carrati frames.

Chessington Cycles (as before). Soma and Maruishi bikes from Japan.

Cycles Peugeot (Edison Road, Bedford). Importers of famous French-made Peugot bikes and tandems for racing, touring and commuting, plus small-wheelers.

IRB (Import & Export) (Charlton Church Lane, London SE7). Importers of Saba bike frames from Italy and other equipment.

Moorland Cycles (as before). Gitane bikes and tandems from France.

Steyr–Daimler–Puch (Lower Parliament Street, Nottingham). Austrian-made Puch small-wheelers and sports bikes, and Austro-Daimler racing and lightweight bikes.

Tigg Sports (Emerson Park, Hornchurch, Essex), Importers of Italian lightweight bicycles, including Colnago.

Universal Cycles (Arterial Road, Rayleigh, Essex). Polish-made range of small-wheelers, sports and touring bikes.

Yung Bicycle Co (Wordsworth Road, Rugby, Warwicks). Range of sports, touring and children's bikes from South Korea.

APPENDIX FIVE

Books, Magazines and Guides

BOOKS ON TOURING

Bikepacking for Beginners by Robin Adshead (£3·25, Oxford Illustrated Press, 1978). Detailed advice on what to take and where to go for cycle touring and camping.

Bicycle Touring in Europe by Karen and Gary Hawkins (£3·25, Sedgwick & Jackson, London, 1974). Guide book and advice on touring areas in Britain and Continent.

Bike and Hike by J. Sydney Jones (£1·95, Oxford Illustrated Press, 1977). Guide book on routes through ten areas of Great Britain and Eire.

Adventure Cycling in Britain by Tim Hughes (£5.95, Blandford Press, Poole, Dorset, 1978). Comprehensive guide to cycle touring in Great Britain, with section on specific routes.

Cycling Book of Tours. (Temple Press – out of print). Guide to 40 routes for tours of between seven and 14 days in British Isles.

Cycling Touring Guides by Harold Briercliffe (Temple Press – out of print). Nine guide books to Great Britain and Ireland.

International Bicycle Touring (Bike World Magazine – U.S.A. Available from Selpress Books at £1·65, 16 Berkeley Street, London W1). American book on touring hints for Europe and rest of world.

England by Bicycle by Frederick Alderson (£1·75, David & Charles). An account of a cycling tour around England by the author.

On Your Bike! A guide to cycling in London. (30p, Friends of the Earth, 93 Lexham Gardens, London W8.) Includes 19 pages of recommended back-street routes for cycling through London.

BOOKS ON MAINTENANCE

All about Bikes and Bicycling by Max Alth (£3·60, Bailey Brothers and Swinton, Folkestone, 1972). Detailed drawings and instructions on repairs and maintenance.

Richard's Bicycle Book by Richard Ballantine (£1·50, Pan Books, 1977). Advice on equipment and bicycles. Section on maintenance.

Readers Digest Basic Guide: The Maintenance of Bicycles – and mopeds (50p, Readers Digest Association, 1975). Detailed drawings on each basic part of bicycle with maintenance notes.

The Raleigh Book of Cycling edited by R. C. Shaw (£1·25, Sphere Books, London WC1, 1978). Useful sections on maintenance and repairs, and assembling a lightweight bike.

Halfords' Guide to Bicycle Maintenance and Repairs (75p).

REFERENCE BOOKS

Cycling (50p, Know the Game series, EP Publishing, Bradford).

Cycle Racing by John Wilcockson (50p, Know the Game series, EP Publishing, Bradford).

Cycle Touring in Europe by Peter Knottley (£2.95, Constable & Co., London, 1975). Practical advice on touring on the continent of Europe.

The Guinness Guide to Bicycling by Jean Durry (£8·50, Guinness Superlatives, 1977).

Cycle Racing: Train to win by Les Woodland (£4·75, Pelham Books, 1975).

Cycle Racing and Touring by Les Woodland (£3·50, Pelham Books, 1976).

Cycling by Frederick Alderson (65p, Futura Publications, 110 Warner Road, London SE5; 1977).

Teach Yourself Cycling by R. C. Shaw (40p, Teach Yourself Books).

Cycling Manual by John R. Way (Temple Press Books – out of print).

British Cycling Federation Handbook (published annually, 1978 edition costs 90p, BCF, 70 Brompton Road, London SW3).

MAGAZINES AND GUIDES

Bicycle Buyers Guide. Sportscene Publishers, 14 Rathbone Place, London W1. Comprehensive guide to new bicycles available on British market, with test reports and comments. Also up-to-date information on trends in leisure and racing aspects of cycling. Published twice a year. 75p.

Cycling. IPC Specialist Press, Throwley House, Sutton, Surrey. Newspaper for cycling sport with racing bias. Touring articles and information. Useful classified section with lists of secondhand lightweight bikes and mail order companies. Published weekly. 25p.

Bicycling Magazine (American). 33 East Minor St, Emmaus, Pa 18049, U.S.A. Glossy colour magazine, that includes extensive information of technical nature on bikes, equipment, touring and medical problems associated with cycling. Published monthly. Available in U.K. (60p) or by subscription.

Bike World Magazine (American). 1400 Stierlin Road, Mountain View, California. Similar to *Bicycling*, but more emphasis on participation in touring and racing. Published bi-monthly. Available on subscription.

Cycletouring. Journal of the Cyclists Touring Club. Published bi-monthly. Available to members. Mainly information and articles on touring in Britain and Europe. Latest information on touring events.

APPENDIX SIX

Useful Addresses

British Cycling Bureau, Stanhope House, Stanhope Place, London W2 (Tel: 01-262 4951).

Sponsored by the British cycle manufacturers, this body exists to help the public with queries about buying bicycles, where to buy and where to obtain other information. Has compiled list of shops that hire out bicycles in Great Britain.

British Cycling Federation, 70 Brompton Road, London SW3 (Tel: 01-584 6706).

Internationally recognised body for governing cycle racing in Great Britain. Offers touring information, free third party insurance and legal aid to members. Handbook lists clubs, repairers and catering establishments.

British Cyclo-Cross Association. National Secretary: 8, Bellam Road, Hampton Magna, Warwick (Tel: 0926-43116).

See page 65.

Cyclists' Touring Club, 69 Meadrow, Godalming, Surrey (Tel: 048 68 7217).

Members receive free third party insurance and legal aid, touring information, adventure holidays, British and overseas tours, local runs and social activities and a bi-monthly magazine (*Cycletouring*).

English Schools Cycling Association. Gen. Sec., 22 Quaves Lane, Bungay, Suffolk.

Membership open to schools and individual school pupils. Object is "to offer cycling to pupils as a recreation and sport, thereby improving their roadcraft and developing their fitness".

Friends of the Earth, 9 Poland Street, London W1 (Tel: 01-434 1684).

National environmental group campaigning for a more rational transport policy, with particular emphasis on use of bicycles. Provides information on cycling in towns at local level.

Road Time Trials Council. National Secretary: Dallacre, Mill Road, Yarwell, Peterborough, Northants.

See page 65.

Tandem Club, 25 Hendred Way, Abingdon, Oxon.

Encourages tandem cycling by organising touring events, providing a spare parts service and publishing a bi-monthly magazine.

Veterans Time Trial Association. Hon. Sec., 137 Glenwood Avenue, Westcliffe-on-Sea, Essex (Tel: Southend-on-Sea 331362).

Provides members with a regular programme of time trial racing, with standard time awards and overall championship competition.

Viking Schools Challenge, Caledonian House, Tatton Street, Knutsford, Cheshire (Tel: 0565-53673).

See page 66.

Youth Hostels Association (England and Wales), Trevelyan House, St Stephens Hill, St Albans, Herts (Tel: St Albans 55215).

Open to all age groups, providing a network of inexpensive accommodation in England and Wales, and providing information on hostels overseas and in other parts of British Isles. YHA shop in London sells specially equipped touring bicycles, plus all other touring requirements and travel facilities.